francine coffey's celebrity sewing bee

francine coffey

harper & row, publishers   new york · evanston · san francisco · london

Color photographs in Part One were taken directly from television tapes recorded live at KTLA-TV in Hollywood, California, and TV studios in New York.

FRANCINE COFFEY'S CELEBRITY SEWING BEE. Copyright © 1974 by Francine Coffey. All rights reserved. Printed in the United States of America. No part of this book may be used or reproduced in any manner whatsoever without written permission except in the case of brief quotations embodied in critical articles and reviews. For information address Harper & Row, Publishers, Inc., 10 East 53rd Street, New York, N.Y. 10022. Published simultaneously in Canada by Fitzhenry & Whiteside Limited, Toronto.

FIRST EDITION

Designed by C. Linda Dingler

Sketches by Merle Altman Wechsler

Library of Congress Cataloging in Publication Data
Coffey, Francine.
    Francine Coffey's celebrity sewing bee.

    1. Sewing. I. Title. II. Title: Celebrity sewing bee.
TT705.C72   1974   646.4   73–18649
ISBN 0–06–010822–3

To my mother,

the

super sewing star

of all time

contents

acknowledgments

You don't ever do an enormous project like a book alone. To a large degree this book is a reflection of the fine and talented people who worked with me. The samples photographed for *Celebrity Sewing Bee* with few exceptions were made by one extremely talented young lady, Merle Altman. She not only understood what was wanted, she came in with the sample even better than I thought it could be done! She also delighted us with the sketches for this book, and when a goodie box came in from Merle it was always the high point of the day.

The second person deeply involved is my secretary, Anne Gatehouse, who is one of the all-time-great worker bees. She sticks to a project like you wouldn't believe, and I guess I should consider it a compliment that people are always trying to hire her away from me. She typed all the words and suffered through doing all the graph paper sketches, and what I shall miss most is her bugging me for more pages.

Ginny Lubrano, another dear friend, searched out some super ideas for the book and Jean Colbert gave it all her eagle eye once over. Not to be left out, there are men to be thanked as well. Certainly Isaac M. Singer, who made home sewing possible, my boss Ted Trevorrow, who encouraged me, and lastly, my husband, Patrick Joyce, whose Irish gift for language always provided the right word.

F.C.

"To do a common thing uncommonly well brings success."

Harland Sanders

part one   francine tells what the fashion biz is *really* all about

You might wonder how a girl from Saint Louis, Missouri, gets a job in the high-fashion world of Paris and then somehow or other ends up in Hollywood teaching movie stars to sew, and on national TV, no less! I can hear you saying to yourself, "There has to be a story behind this," and believe me, there is. And the story even surprises me sometimes because I never had any thought of being on TV and working with movie stars. One thing is for certain. If you open yourself up to what life hands you, it will hand you the darnedest things.

It all really started with my great-grandmother's Singer sewing machine when I was eight years old. That's when my mother and grandmother taught me to sew. I started off with doll clothes for a blond-haired blue-eyed doll named Sonja, who had come at Christmas time with her very own evening gown, skating outfit, brassiere and girdle. I don't know who designed that doll's wardrobe but I would have agreed with Sonja if she had said, "I don't have a thing to wear!"

The first garment I made for Sonja was a pleated skirt; my grandmother made a matching blouse. (If you're a home sewer I don't need to tell you I took the easier one.) Then I made her a nightgown because a doll is only fun if you can dress and undress her and, well, Sonja became the best-dressed doll on the block. My little friends Joanne, Patsy and Doris took note and what ensued was the female version of card swapping, only we swapped scraps of fabric from our mothers' scrap boxes. We used to sit for hours in a cool basement during the Saint Louis summertime trading pieces of inexpensive cotton scraps left over from something our mothers had made for themselves or one of us. It was pure heaven! Some of the fabrics were so bright and colorful you just knew they would make great doll clothes. At the end of that summer my brother nicknamed me "Scraphappy," which I hated but ignored because at that age all men were pure pests.

When I was nine my grandmother started

3

Then work in department store fashion offices in the summertime. With the work experience and the French degree, you'll be all set." And that's exactly what I did.

My first real job to speak of was working for the most talented lady I have ever known. Her name was Marjorie Wilten and she was the fashion director of Stix, Baer & Fuller department store in downtown Saint Louis.

(Right after graduate school I had been a photographer's model in Miami, Florida. It was great fun and there was a lot of work because Miami got a good share of television commercials during the winter months and also handled the travel brochures for all the Bahamian islands. So one day I was off to be photographed in Saint Petersburg for the Florida tourist commission and the next day it was to Nassau or Harbour Island to play the happy vacationer for the Bahamian tourist bureau.

I must admit it was always a thrill to get my pay check in an envelope stamped with a crest of the British government and, under it, the words "In Her Majesty's Service." But modeling is the same thing over and over day after day and I decided to move on and learn more about the fashion business. That's where Marjorie Wilten came in.)

I was home on vacation and my mother said she had heard that Marjorie Wilten was now fashion director of Stix, and if I wanted to learn, she was the person to learn under. How right she was. Mrs. Wilten was one of the most talented people I'll ever have the privilege to know. She came from a well-to-do family but an unusual one. Her father was stage manager for the Ziegfeld Follies and she was born in a trunk, or so she said. She had seen some of the most unusual stage settings of all times, so when she described her vision of a new fashion show runway, "a conical type, like the inside of a shell that circles up to the sky," you looked at her as if she were crazy, and yet, if you just hung around long enough, you saw that runway built with fans blowing the models' long chiffon gowns as they floated down it. (Though the runway was carpeted with rubber matting, a beautiful red-haired model named Carolyn slipped and fell on it once during a show, and was heard to comment after that, "It's a conical blankety-blank, *that's* what it is!")

Marjorie Wilten had a group of six fashion coordinators who helped her do all the shows for the store. I became one of them because I naïvely called up the personnel office of Stix and said I wanted to work for Mrs. Wilten. They said there was no job, but I said I didn't care, I just wanted to meet Mrs. Wilten. Maybe in the future there would be a job. I did get my interview and I was hired; there *was* a job in the future, about ten months away. Stix was opening a branch store named River Roads and they needed a fashion coordinator. I became that coordinator, but first I trained downtown under Mrs. Wilten.

I don't think anyone is ever quite ready for what happens to her on her first day of work on a new job. I certainly wasn't. My first assignment was to get all the traffic stopped around the downtown store for an entire Saturday. Marjorie Wilten had decided she wanted to have a block party with dancing in the streets, outdoor cafés and high school jazz groups playing throughout the day. The *how* of how things got done didn't matter to her—just get it done, even if you have to call the mayor to stop the busy downtown traffic. It's funny, but I, who thought then that she was one nutty lady, am the same way today. When I give an assignment I don't want to hear about how you have to go about getting it done; just do it. Some people, with that inner creative drive, take the ball and run. Others can't function that way, so you learn to give them projects with defined steps, where the end is in sight from the beginning.

When you meet people who are the "Give me a challenge!" type, you can usually see a certain spark in their eye. Once I was doing a fashion show at Higbee's department store in Cleveland, and I met a pair of sensationally talented young people running the fabric department. Gary Crissey was the buyer and Eleanor Erwine his assistant. The department had fabric in baskets, fabric in barrels, fabric displayed in most unusual and charming ways. On our way to get coffee, Eleanor spied some armoires in the furniture department, and we agreed one would house fabric beautifully. Now furniture department people don't think much of helping out anyone, especially fabric department people, so I was really quite surprised the next morning when I went into the fabric department and there was an armoire, chock full of fabrics. I don't know how she did it. She's a tiny five foot two but I have the feeling that after store hours (before they stopped the escalators) she and Gary . . . well, it sure didn't get there by itself! They laugh about it still, but they won't tell how they did it.

To get back to Marjorie Wilten, she held a staff meeting every Monday morning in her office, at which she would hand out assignments for the coming week. There were a lot of shows to get on runways, both in and out of the store (ladies' clubs, country clubs and the like), as well as daily tearoom modeling. My first show was with the junior high school board models, preteen girls chosen from different schools to model clothes on Saturday. It was quite an honor to be on a board and great experience for them. There were also high school and college modeling boards. Well, I'm here to tell you the worst people in the world to fit are preteens. They are all tummy with no shoulders, they fall over anything more than one inch off the floor and are so insecure and unsure of themselves that only their parents could love them. Children, grandmothers, fat ladies—anyone is easier to fit and handle than a preteen. They also usually have a mouthful of braces and freckles to match. Anyway, there I was with twenty-seven kids. I had to fit them, choose their accessories, get them accustomed to their outfits and the runway (without falling off) and then put on the show with all the hoopla of show biz—music, lights, action, etc.—and lastly I had to be commentator. I stared at my assignment for a long time, thinking: How on earth do you put on a fashion show? Finally, one of the other coordinators took me by the hand and led me to the preteen department. I learned you put clothes together in color groups—e.g., red/white/blue—and have all the models in one color group come out on the stage at the same time to achieve some kind of impact. You do spiffy, bright-colored clothes first so the music can be lively and get everyone emotionally up for what they are going to see. You put your worst group of garments in the middle of the show because people remember better what they see first and last. You change your music according to the type of garment on the runway: pretty music for evening gowns, peppy music for sportswear, and so forth. You are also responsible for the printing of programs, the placing of an ad in the newspaper, the printing and distribution of tickets and the hiring of dressers to help the models make quick changes. Lastly, when the final garment has gone down the runway—hopefully none of them has been worn backward—you go backstage, tell all the models how great they were and then start returning all the clothes and accessories to their respective departments so they can be sold because of that wonderful show you put on. Sounds like a lot of work? It is, and the person who said, "You have to be part horse

The author backstage, fitting a model for a fashion show (left), and onstage, doing the commentary.

and part human to be in the fashion business," sure knew what he or she was talking about. You lug the clothes around, move the racks, even run the freight elevator, all to get a show on the runway, and believe me, it's not glamorous. It is exciting and fun, however, and I've never had a morning when I didn't want to get up and go to work!

Marjorie Wilten was more to me than just a talented, eccentric boss. She sat me down behind a closed door in her office once and told me how to get department store people to do things for you. Whether they are paid to help you or not doesn't make any difference. Sometimes the most important person in your life at the moment is the gal who presses show clothes. If she won't move, you don't get your show on the runway. So you go into the pressing room, pulling a rack of clothes behind you, and the first thing you ask is, "How are you feeling today?" If the

reply is negative, you inquire about her lumbago or her alcoholic husband or her son who is a juvenile delinquent. It would appear that the last thing you had on your mind was to get the clothes pressed. After five minutes of small talk you ask her to do you a favor. Could she get these clothes pressed for you by such and such a time? She will almost always say she doesn't know; leave the clothes and she'll see what she can do. When you come back for them, they are always ready. Marjorie Wilten's whole approach in getting anybody to do anything was to make them feel as if you couldn't do your job without their help. Amazing how well it works . . . and of course I still use it today.

There are always disasters in the fashion-show business but it's amazing how little the public notices them. And of course one of the best ways to learn is through disasters. I remember a time when this grand lady boss of mine decided to stage the annual college show (which had become a small Broadway musical because the models danced and sang) in the American Theater in downtown Saint Louis. Now that is a big theater seating two thousand people and the date was to be August 6. We believed the theater manager when he said he would start the air-conditioning unit at 8 A.M. so that it would be cool by afternoon for the show.

Rule No. 1, learned from an unknowledgeable theater manager: Don't believe anyone when he tells you a theater of that size needs only six hours to cool off.

By 2 P.M., show time, it was 95 degrees outside and 107 degrees in the theater. The sixty college models, all wearing winter woolens, were dropping like flies backstage. We stripped them down, and right before they were to go on, did a fast dress act.

But that wasn't the only problem. The sound wasn't working well and Marjorie Wilten's commentary couldn't be heard. Finally, the show was over, much to everyone's relief, and I went out on stage. Marjorie Wilten hadn't moved from the high stool on which she was perched. I looked at her and through clenched teeth she gritted, "Will somebody get me down off of here?" It seems she had fallen on the steps leading up to the microphone, had picked herself up and struggled to the stool where she sat while doing the commentary for the show. It also seems she had broken both kneecaps when she fell and as the doctor said afterward, how she got to the stool he'd never know, but two thousand people saw her do it and could attest to it. She knew she had hurt something but of course the show must go on was always her motto . . . and it did! (A hospital bed and both legs in casts strung up to the ceiling didn't stop her either. Staff meetings were held as usual in her hospital room, shows were assigned, schedules met

and all the while she was dressed in the height of fashion bed-jacket-wise.)

Stix, Baer & Fuller was the first department store in America to find and hire a black female model. They had been looking for one for two years and they found just the right person on the University of Missouri campus. She was a twenty-one-year-old girl named Diane White, who was a drama major and very attractive. Her hair was pulled back in a chignon and she had a certain sense of herself. She would need that too, because the going was not going to be easy for her. We first used Diane in the store for tearoom modeling. Her job was to go up to tables in the tearoom and tell customers what department her dress came from and how much it cost. It's a lovely and inexpensive way of getting your merchandise before the eyes of the customers while they are held captive by a chicken salad sandwich.

The Stix tearoom was a long, rectangular room and as Diane entered that first time (this was before blacks were even allowed to eat there) silence descended—that is, forks dropped but mouths were shut. As she proceeded down the center of the room, more silence but then a distinct buzzing started that followed the silence. It was an undulating wave of silence followed by one of buzzing. She was scared to death and we were scared to death. A few customers left, saying they would never set foot in Stix, Baer & Fuller again, but of course the majority remained and Diane continued tearoom modeling. Things went along quite smoothly until the day in December when we were showing cruise wear and the models had put on Man Tan or Pale Male to give their arms and legs some color for the clothes. Well, Diane went out and did her first tour of the tearoom, returning in what I thought was tears until I realized she was laughing so hard she couldn't speak. After she got control of herself, she said that when she had finished her spiel at a table where two little old ladies were seated, one of them said to her how pretty she looked and then, "Tell me, dear, where did you go to get your tan? All the girls have lovely tans but yours looks the *nicest!*" From then on we used to tease Diane by telling her to go sit out in the sun, as she wasn't dark enough! Diane White went on from modeling to become this country's and Saint Louis's first black female TV weather forecaster and she does that job to this day.

I guess the worst kind of show to put on is a traveling show with a "star." Usually a traveling show is a collection of garments that arrive at your store with accessories. Once you've done the show, you ship the garments on to the next store. With a "star" traveling show, that's not the case. You hire a limousine, meet the star at the airport, get a suite at a hotel, flowers in the room, etc. It's a lot of extra work and coddling that doesn't seem necessary because people are people, but you get the typed sheet as to what the star's demands are (down to a certain brand of chewing gum in the hotel room, no less) and you do it. Sometimes, though, you are made to realize that people are people and stars are stars. For instance, Gloria Swanson, who had a line of clothes bearing her name, traveled with a personal maid and a personal potty. We were told that she wouldn't use any public facilities and therefore to make her dressing room close enough to the ladies' room so her maid could empty her potty!

Joan Crawford got off a plane to do a show wearing ankle-strap black suede high heels and a 1940s padded-shoulder suit. I had been told to write a commentary for her to deliver so I listed each dress, its cost, the model's name and the department where it could be found and handed the notebook to her. She looked at it and asked where the commentary was. I realized she couldn't speak unless every "and," "the" and "but" was written on the page for her. I was doubly shocked when she threw the notebook at me and screamed that I was trying to ruin her. You can see why department store fashion offices sometimes groan when a star show is on the schedule.

Besides stars giving a performance when you least expect it, children and animals do the same. I've had children turn upside down to show off lace on their panties because they thought that was the most important thing to show and sometimes they have even taken them off so everyone could get a closer look.

I've also hired Afghan dogs and stupidly placed potted palm trees on the stage. While the dogs waited with their mistresses for their turn to go down the runway, you can imagine what they did with the palms . . . at the Waldorf Astoria in New York, no less. Also, I've learned that when children and animals are on a runway, *nobody* looks at the clothes.

Having learned how to put on fashion shows, I decided it was time to go to Paris and do what I had always dreamed of doing: work in the world of Parisian high fashion. I had no contacts, relatives or friends in Europe whatsoever. I was your typical naïve, optimistic American. And I had a rude awakening.

I landed in Paris on a cold January day and had trouble understanding the customs officer. I didn't think much about it until I couldn't handle the accent of the taxicab driver. Then it dawned on me that I had studied book French all those years in college and everybody here spoke either slang or a mixture of the two. I spent two whole weeks in Paris barely getting by and getting madder by the day thinking of the time spent in college and how ill prepared I was to handle the street French. What good is it to know the history, literature and politics of a country when you can't speak to its people? So I decided to go to Switzerland, where I had to research and write a thesis for a master's degree back in the States. I had written the administration at the University of Lausanne telling them I had chosen Switzerland's foremost author, Charles Ferdinand Ramuz, to do my thesis on and would I be able to work on it at the university? I was told that all the original manuscripts of Charles Ferdinand Ramuz were in their keeping at the university library and I would be most welcome to them. I had chosen this man because no American had written about him before. Most of his books had never been printed in English and I would have to go to Lausanne (he had lived nearby in Pully) to do the work. Concerning the thesis, nothing was more distasteful to me than doing a thesis that involved hours of research time knowing that a hundred or more people had chosen the same subject and that all their efforts were relegated to the microfilm file in the end anyway. One graduate school professor had looked at me and said wearily, "Everything has been done before. Nothing is new." Well, I had other thoughts and set out to accomplish what only a naïve American can.

I took the Paris-Lausanne express train, tipping the French porter well when he said he had put my bags next to a handsome young man on the train. The man turned out to be sixty-five if a day and a hunchback to boot, and all I could think of that porter was "how typically French." I remembered a day tour to Versailles during which the middle-aged Canadian next to me on the bus cried and told me he had lost his wife—that is, she had left Montreal one week before him and they were supposed to meet in Paris. It had been one month and he had still not been able to locate her. When he went to the French authorities and told them he had lost his wife, the official said, *"Comme c'est charmant!"* (How charming!)

At any rate, I quietly rode the five hours to Lausanne wondering what was waiting for me in Switzerland. Because of my limitations in speaking "street French," I had not talked to anyone for almost a month. It was cold and dreary and I was more than just a little homesick. To sum it up, I was ready to turn around and go back home. But the train jolted to a stop in Switzerland and, with a lump in my throat, I carried my suitcase up the hill from the station, stopping in front of the first hotel I saw, Hotel des Palmiers. I inquired about a room and after the clerk said yes, he added, "It's amazing, but you're the forty-sixth American to check in today." I immediately saw the words of the Pledge of Allegiance, "The Star-Spangled Banner," Lincoln's Gettysburg Address and the last paragraph of the Declaration of Independence swim before my eyes. The other Americans, I was soon to find out, were young soldiers stationed in France, who had come to Switzerland on a skiing holiday. I walked into the dining room and forty-five pairs of American eyes turned and stared. I was the first American girl they had seen in over a year. The waitress soon brought a pencil-scrawled note that said, "Are you by any chance an American?" I answered with one word in block letters and with that forty-five soldiers descended on me.

What were the girls wearing back home? What was the latest song? Who was the newest popular singer? etc., etc., until four o'clock in the morning. The restaurant closed at midnight and we sat on the stairs of the hotel until finally I had no voice left. Their commanding officer said I could go only if I promised to join them for two days of skiing at Rochers de Naye. I did, we got snowed in, and more hours and hours and hours of conversation ensued about America.

Rule No. 2: No one, but no one, knows

what this country is all about until he or she *leaves* it.

The next few weeks in Lausanne were filled with new experiences that were awe inspiring (hearing the Lord's Prayer spoken in French), trying (looking for a roommate and an apartment to share through the Lausanne *Tribune*) and downright disgusting (finding out that the bottle of wine you bought is really vinegar because the shopkeeper couldn't understand your Americanized French).

But I did find two roommates. Siri, Norwegian and American by birth, was my age and was learning her fourth language. She had never bothered with American universities. She just spent a year in each country where she wanted to learn the language, got a job doing most anything and at the end of her year packed her bags to move on because she had another language under her belt. Now *that's* the way to learn languages! The other roommate was an Austrian girl, who spoke only German. As I didn't speak a word of German, when Siri wasn't around our conversation was uninspiring, to say the least. I slept in the same bed with her, and it's amazing how far away from a person you feel when you can't even say, "Sweet dreams."

I enrolled in a crash course of idiomatic French, started research on my thesis at the university library and went down to the local department store, Innovation, hopefully to get some kind of work. Luckily it was the spring fashion-show season and I was hired as a model. Do you have any idea how frustrating it is when you have forty-five seconds for a change and you can't even tell your dresser to please unzip you? Whoever learns *that* phrase in a French class?

The spring show season ended and I realized that I had learned more French while working than I had in my classes. So I decided to go to the personnel office and ask if they had any job at all, as that was the best way for me to learn to speak the language. Luckily, they were opening a branch store in Montreux, a resort town about forty-five minutes away from Lausanne, and they needed an interpreter for the English and American tourists who would be visiting during the summer months. I got the job and the first thing we did was stock the store. It couldn't have been better for me as each day I was put in a different department. I would take out my little black notebook and write the French name of every item I was putting in stock. The department managers helped and by the end of that month I knew the French word for every item found in a department store, from a mourning button to a garbage can.

The tourists descended like a Swiss avalanche, and I have never worked so hard in my life. I had my own bell on the store buzzer system and when I heard that bell, I went to the nearest telephone, picked it up and a voice would say what department I was needed in. There were seventy Swiss employees in the store and perhaps twenty could make a sale to an English-speaking customer without any help from an interpreter. The rest . . . well, the work was six days a week and on Sunday, the seventh, you couldn't have got me out of bed if you had tried. But I learned the language and now I have the fondest memories of the little town of Montreux and of some of the people who vacationed there.

One person I will never forget is Mrs. Ronald Colman, who was eighty years plus and talked lovingly of "Ronnie" even though her marriage to him had lasted only two years. She had never remarried and often reminisced about him and the time when she was a Blue Belle dancing girl in London. She also gave advice on getting married, and that was to marry three times in your lifetime and marry better financially each time. She

12

daughters of wealthy countesses and baronesses come in to help sell as a lark, to see what it's like in a Paris couture house, and they don't work for a salary. They bring their friends, who buy, and then usually quit after one collection. I thanked Madame Benjamin, saying I didn't think my concierge would accept a glory check, and was out on the street, my joy terribly short-lived.

I went to the other nine major couture houses but they all had one story and it was the same. "We can't hire you because you don't have a French working permit." Then I would go to the French government and they would say, "We can't give you a working permit because you don't have a job." It is known as the old run-around, and it is designed to keep foreigners from getting a job. Their own people need the work and they don't feel kindly inclined to help anyone else. Besides foreign people not being able to get working permits, foreign businesses can't get them either. I had read about the problems of a young Italian couturier, Roberto Capucci, in *Women's Wear Daily* while I was at Stix, Baer & Fuller. He had been trying to open a house of *haute couture* in Paris for two years and even though he was very successful in Rome, he (or rather, his sister) couldn't get a permit to open in Paris. When I arrived in Paris, he had just managed to open his couture house, and I thought that if anybody would understand my plight, it would be he.

So I got all dressed up and went to see Roberto Capucci. I think the head *vendeuse* thought I was a wealthy American client (yes, Europeans still think *all* Americans are wealthy) and I was led into his office. I simply stated that they were trying to keep me out as they had tried to keep him out and that I would work for nothing for three months doing anything, even picking up pins, if he would hire me so I could get a French working permit. He laughed, said

something about American ingenuity and *hired* me. I was to be his press attaché, an unusual job in itself.

There are about seven hundred fashion journalists invited to Paris twice a year to cover the couture collections. It is the job of a press attaché to send out the invitations and then book these journalists into showings according to their nationality and the importance of their country press-wise and dollar-/or franc-wise. Because Capucci was an Italian house, the Italian press saw the collection first; then because the house was in Paris and he wanted to cultivate the good will of the French, the French press was invited next; then came the Americans and Germans because of their buying power and so on down the line. I became aware of certain characteristics of these groups. The English smoke the most, the Germans have an overabundance of galoshes, umbrellas and packages with them and the Italians never stop talking, not even during the show. The Italians are also the most charming. They call you by your first name, kiss your hand and then tell you that you are unorganized if you are five minutes late in getting a dress to them to be photographed even though they were five hours late in returning dresses the day before!

Besides inviting all the journalists, press people are responsible for loaning the show garments out every night to be photographed by the fashion magazine people. The fashion-show collection (about 225 garments) is shown once a day and after the two-hour show is over, the garments are on loan for photography purposes only. They must be returned that night so they are available for the show the next day. The press attaché's job is to keep a very neat "Where They Are" book so that she doesn't misplace a garment—or a "creation," as they are called by the French. It is also her job to stay at the house (all night, if necessary) until the last creation is returned. It is a grueling few weeks, to say the least.

I guess the thing that surprised me most was that, in Paris, models wear no bra while working a show. Also, more often than not, men, such as assistant designers, designers, etc., help dress the girls during the show. While I was in Paris there were only two other Americans in the fashion business there. One was a nineteen-year-old Texas girl modeling for the house of Nina Ricci and the other was a husky ex-marine who was assistant designer to Guy Laroche. We would meet every three months or so to have a Cinzano and talk about how bad living conditions were in Paris. (We all had cardboard in our shoes to cover the holes, which was fine except on rainy days.) Bill would invariably be late and as he rushed up he would apologize, saying how he had got stuck zipping and unzipping all those models for the show. I would laugh to myself, thinking that any other red-blooded ex-marine would love the opportunity, but Bill thought that was beneath him.

There is a great deal of homosexuality in the fashion world and one of the saddest people I ever encountered in Paris was a very talented young hairdresser from Chicago who had got a job at the most famous and prestigious hair-dressing establishment in France. It was the dream of a lifetime for him but it was all shattered when he was invited for the weekend to the country house of his boss and in no uncertain terms was told he would either play the game or he wouldn't keep his job. He had to make a decision that would affect him for a lifetime.

Models in Paris are very thin, even skinny, young women. When I first saw a group of models undressed I was ready to call CARE and tell them about a new disaster area. Each girl is a walking advertisement for Bones, Incorporated. Yet they almost all say

they *watch* their weight. Some take pills to get rid of a meal once they have eaten it and others exist on salads with no dressing and hot tea laced with lots of sugar. Of course they faint every once in a while during work but they are just rolled over to the side of the *cabine* until they come to and are able to finish the show. They also do things to themselves to achieve a certain look. For instance, some have their back molars pulled for that hollow-cheeked look. For a flat bosom, some have *the* operation or else bind themselves much as you would wrap a mummy. You may think this is all terrible but it's an everyday happening in the French fashion world. Every once in a while—not a daily happening, fortunately—you hear of a model who is no longer hired because of her age and commits suicide. Jobs are not plentiful in Paris and a model usually has had little formal education and is not trained to do anything else. When her modeling days are over, unless she has married, she can become a sales clerk and that's about it. Also, contrary to what you may think, models in couture houses make very little money. They are allowed to borrow clothes from the house when they have a date for a ball, an embassy party, etc., as that helps to advertise the house, but they are not allowed to keep these clothes. Some houses, like Chanel, did give the models one garment from the Spring/Summer collection and one from the Fall/Winter collection, because it would not help the house to have the models dressed poorly once they walked out the front door. Of course the clothes are so expensive (a daytime dress may start at a thousand dollars) models would never be able to buy them. I think that by now you can see it's definitely not as glamorous a life as it seems.

The fashion business in Paris is known in French as the world of *haute couture. Haute* means "high" or "fine" and *couture* means "seam"; therefore, the whole business of French fashion is based on some pretty fine seams. They don't design simple anything. If it looks simple it has a maze of seamed constructions underneath to help it look that way. Most people buy couture because of the intricate seams and fine hand-sewn details. Of course the fabrics are glorious and the design taste exquisite . . . most of the time. Sometimes you'll have a dress in the collection that has, say, a pair of giant red lips sewn across it . . . for fun. The designer is having a laugh and expects you to do the same. However, some people take Paris fashion so seriously that they think they must follow everything. They look upon French couture designers as if their word is The Word, but I never did meet a god the whole time I was there. I only met talented, bright, sensitive and sometimes ordinary people who have as much trouble deciding where to put the bow as you or I. They just have more time allowed them to do something than we do here. With our fast way of mass producing (and it's faster to copy than to create something), we just copy. That's all there is to it. I guess nothing puts things in proper perspective as much as working on the other side of the fence, if you know what I mean.

Collections are expensive to make and French couture houses have a hard time keeping from going under when they have a collection or two that are not well received by the press or paying clients. So they live on money made from the sale of perfume. As soon as a house is established, it comes out with a fragrance, as there is a great deal of profit in perfume. However, there is no free publicity in it. Therefore, the couture part of the house gets the free publicity and that helps keep the perfume sales up. After the Second World War, Coco Chanel came back and opened her house of couture because her perfume sales had fallen off. She received a tremendous amount of publicity from her couture collections and in no time the perfume sales were higher than ever.

Coco Chanel was perhaps one of the most talented designers the French couture has ever produced. You couldn't help but love her and yet you felt as if you were in the presence of a smoldering volcano that could erupt at any moment. She perched on the winding staircase of the house to watch the collection and nobody missed the feel of her eye. I always loved her models and her clothes. They looked so fresh and so feminine that one immediately thought of the old saying "There are a few things that never go out of style and a feminine woman is one of them."

Mademoiselle Chanel's real first name was Gabrielle, but the story goes that she was nicknamed Cocorico when she was young and it was shortened to Coco as she grew older. She started making hats for wealthy society women and moved on to making clothes. She was the designer who first put women in pants and costume jewelry, first put artificial gardenias on clothes, designed the first sling-back shoe and shoulder-strap handbag, the turtleneck sweater, the trench coat, and many more firsts, too numerous to mention here. She was a titanic force in the evolution of clothes for women.

There were always a lot of stories circulating about her. One that I can vouch for concerned a client who complained about her new Chanel suit not being properly pressed. She didn't understand about the softly rolled hem edge that all well-made clothes have. When she said the hem should be pressed flat like a crease, Mademoiselle's dark eyebrows shot up to the top of her head and she said, "My dear, creases only belong in a man's pair of pants!" And you never answered Mademoiselle back either.

I thought that before I left Paris I should get some work experience with a French house so I resigned from Capucci and began making the rounds. It was pretty poor pickings so I decided to try department stores and started off with Les Galeries Lafayette. That was as far as I got because I had an interview that I will remember as long as I live. With the precious work permit now in hand, I filled out an application and waited to be called into the office of the personnel director. He looked the application over and asked if I was living with my parents. I said no, I had a room in a hotel. Then he asked if I was married. Since I had written ''Mademoiselle'' on the application, I thought he was a bit dense, but I said no, I was not and had no plans to be married. Finally he said, "Then you have a lover, somebody who is keeping you?'' My face flushed by then at the questioning, I said most certainly not, and with that he picked up my application, tore it in half, threw it in the nearby waste can and said, ''Then I'm sorry. We can't hire you.'' He went on to explain that girls who were living alone in Paris without a husband or a man to keep them were the ones who stole the most from department stores. If I could produce a paper that somebody was keeping me, then he would reconsider—but not without the paper. I walked out thinking they would never believe this in Saint Louis, Missouri!

By then my funds were at rock bottom. It was either a job or use the return ticket home. I was just about to do the latter when I heard that a new house had opened and that it was backed by American money. The designer's name was Yves Saint Laurent. Going to see him, I walked down the lovely street of Spontini until I came to 18 bis, a beautiful stone building with five or six stories and a lovely winding staircase on the main floor. Instead of Saint Laurent, the *directrice* of the house, Madame de Peyrimoff, came out and asked about my work background. She immediately hired me to

work with the American and English buyers and this time I got a salary. It was $125 a month, which seemed like a bushel of money at the time. I was supposed to help bring in the American dollar because that's what started and would keep Saint Laurent in business until he really got going. The backer was J. Mack Robinson, out of Atlanta, Georgia, and he had taken a very young and talented man in the person of Saint Laurent to start the house. Mind you, he wasn't doing this on pure speculation. Saint Laurent was a well-known young genius. He had been found by Christian Dior in a design school in Paris when he was fourteen and brought to the house of Dior as an apprentice. When Dior died in 1957, everyone knew Saint Laurent was the desired choice of Dior to follow him. He did follow, but the French army intervened to draft him and when he came out in his early twenties, the house of Dior had an older, more established man in the design slot, Marc Bohan. By that time the house of Dior (owned by Marcel Boussac, of washing machine, fabric, etc., fame) was big business. So Saint Laurent was out of a job and it was an American who put him back in the couture game. (When Chanel reopened her house in 1954, the French press panned her but the American press and department store buyers backed her and sent her on her way upward and onward. Thank God for the Americans.)

I was working at YSL from 10 A.M. to 6 P.M. and my eyes were bugging out of my head with what I was seeing. One of the top floors was devoted to the workrooms, where the old type of flatirons were still being used. The techniques were bizarre, to say the least. Seamstresses would put their hands under the hot-water tap, dry them and then with the heat in their hands caress the fold of a collar on a suit to get just the right amount of roll where needed. One per-

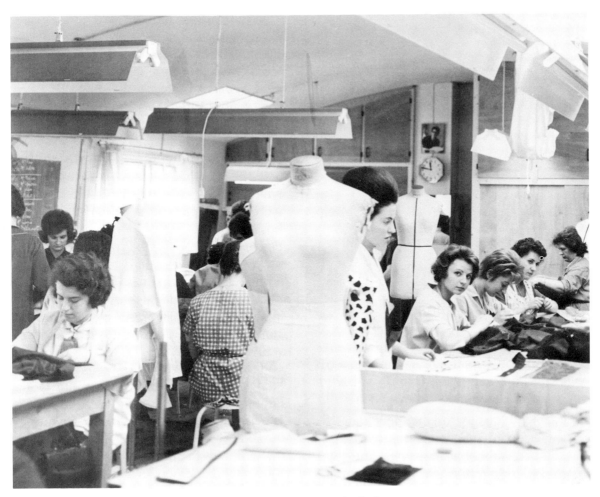

The workrooms at the couture house of Yves Saint Laurent in Paris.

son worked on a garment until it was finished and sometimes it would take an entire week.

Because such loving care was put into these garments, you carried them with just as much care. You were allowed to carry only one garment at a time. If you grabbed a group of clothes over your arm, you would be fired on the spot for the disrespect you showed them. Even today it wounds my soul when I see a well-made jacket hanging on a wire hanger or over the back of a chair. Shape has been pressed into that jacket and

no wire hanger or chair back is going to help retain the shape.

The ground floor of the house contained fabric storage and the house restaurant (a five-course meal was served every day at noon for five francs, or a dollar), the main floor was the salon, boutique and models' *cabine,* and the second floor the office of Saint Laurent and the design room. Next were the workroom floors and the very top floor was the billing office. The house had no elevator and I remember a lot of running up and down stairs. I also remember the

Christian Dior

1 ... jersey écossais beige ... sier voile de laine assorti.

2 Ve... antalon shetland bleu « jeans ». ... crêpe satin écossais assorti.

3 Ve... cachemire naturel. Pantalo... fl... cachemire naturel. Chemi... cr... ... ain façonné ...

4 Veste ... alon et manteau ... an shetland ... be... é.

5 Taille... antalon lainage qua... cuite ... ... louse crêpe de ... Manteau ... nage blanc.

✳ 6 Veste daim bleu. Pantalon jersey ... bleu. Blouse crêpe satin imprimé bleu.

7 Veste mol... ... ge. Pantalon cachem... beige. B... rêpe satin façonné be...

8 Veste ... leu « jeans ». Panta... je... ... rine. Chemisier cr... s... ... leu. Pardessus shetla...

9 ... ne beige garni vison ... ... Pantalon tweed ble... ... mi... atin façonné bleu.

10 Imperm... ne vert garni vison ... vert ... antalon flanelle vert « lod... rêpe satin écossais vert ...

11 Imper... ... terre cuite » garni vis... ... ». Jupe de twill as... ... jersey écossais ...

12 ... ne garni vison ... ... en crêpe de ...

14 Im... ... vison » rouge laque. ... be crêpe de Chine rouge laque.

15 Tailleur tweed chiné, ble... Blouse crêpe de laine assorti.

16 Tailleur jersey éc... ... bleu et brun. Blous... ... sorti.

17 Tailleur shetland ... ... ise crêpe satin écossais...

18 Tailleur she... ... satin écossa...

19 Tailleur ... ... et Blouse crêp... ... é brique.

... Tailleur jersey écossa... « oblique » rouge. Blouse crêpe satin ... ssais assorti.

21 Tailleur pantalon ... cossais « obli- que » vert. Blouse crêpe satin écossais assorti.

22 Tailleur jersey écossais « oblique » « terre cuite ». Blouse crêpe satin écossais assorti.

23 Robe jersey ... ... beige rosé. Paletot lainage ...

24 Manteau ... ... hetland brun. Robe étamine ... ... ssais brun et beige.

25 Manteau ... ... bleu. Veste tweed bleu et ... ... étamine de laine écossai...

26 Paletot la... ... e en shetland bleu « ... ... crêpe satin écossai...

27 Manteau ... ... be flanelle bleu...

28 Mante... ... ...es jersey imp...

29 Mant... ... tweed beige.

30 Robe et manteau tweed marron et blanc.

* "Mink International".

eggshell nested snugly in the other half. Sound easy? Well, it's not, but I thought I might learn the secret, among others, at the Cordon Bleu.

The Cordon Bleu was founded in 1880 by Mademoiselle Martha Distil, not for professional chefs but rather for daughters of upper-class French families. As the years passed, the school acquired a reputation for aspiring gastronomes and men and women have come from all over to study . . . or so said the brochure.

However, I was not prepared for my first day, when my class was herded into a sterile-looking room where we faced a red-faced, potbellied white-hatted French chef —just the kind you read about. We were also greeted by a friendly lobster, who waved his claw when we entered. He wasn't dead yet and he was on the day's menu!

The chef was a real showman. He threw dirty pots and pans to his assistants and never measured, just tossed, guessed, sprinkled and made it all look very easy—until he proceeded to assassinate friend lobster, who had been playing quietly over in the corner with a stale bouillon cube. I had already decided I would never be able to kill a lobster and I will never forget the wiggling he did before the butcher knife pierced his brain—but, as the chef asserted, "One must never purchase a dead lobster." I must admit that twenty minutes later, the assassination and cremation completed, yon lobster reappeared looking most edible, robed in a steaming tomato sauce. So I signed up for more French cooking classes, but do you know, I never did learn to break an egg with one hand.

By now I was ready to come home. The letters from home had been hinting quite openly that I had been abroad long enough. When they started including love notes from the five-year-old boy next door, such as:

Dear Francine,
When are you going to come home so we can play in the dirt?
Love,
Jeff

I knew that it was time. Besides, I was tired of the sixth-floor walk-up, tired of the one shower every ten days (it cost a dollar to take that shower) and tired of sharing the bathroom at the end of the hall every morning with four or five tall African males. They were all diplomatic students at the nearby embassy and wore beautiful striped silk caftans. They completely disregarded me, which made me feel all the more insecure as I stood in line with them in my plain blue terry-cloth housecoat.

I had learned what I had come for plus quite a bit more. I learned that the French love you if you make a fuss. For example, don't ever take the first table offered you in a restaurant. Choose the best table in the room and say you want that one. That shows you consider yourself worthy of the best and they respect anybody who cares about having the best of everything. They also love it when you lose your temper. I did only once but my co-workers looked up and smiled, and one said, "My, she has spirit." I learned that they don't accept foreigners into their circle of friends. I was never inside a French home the entire time I was there. I learned that they love their language with a passion and that was beautiful to me because it is definitely a language to be passionate about. Once a bus driver made me say several times where I wanted to go until I got the accent correct. There was a line of passengers behind me waiting to board the bus but that didn't matter. He was so pleased when I finally got it right that he grinned from ear to ear. I learned that it is not living, merely existing, when you are in a country where you do not have family or friends or a government that you can go to

This is really what it's all about at the Paris high-fashion houses—great-looking clothes whose key word is quality, quality, quality!

for help. Also, the most beautiful city in the world does not keep you entranced when there is no love, warmth or kindness around you.

I boarded the plane to come home and found myself with a Catholic priest on my left and a rabbi on my right. Believe me, I wasn't worried about getting back to the land of milk and honey! Both men, by the way, offered me a sleeping pill for the crossing. They had to lecture when they got to New York and couldn't afford to be tired. I took one and found that is a delightful way to make a crossing. I was so excited when I got off the plane that I didn't notice the frown on the customs officer's face when he looked at my health card. It seems that my smallpox vaccination was no longer valid and he said, "Sorry, we can't let you back in the country . . ." My heart sank. ". . . unless you roll up your sleeve." I did, he vaccinated me and as I was wondering how I was going to pay him with only eight francs in my purse, he said, "It's free." I had just come from a continent where you were charged for ice cubes, for the use of a mirror to comb your hair, for paper shopping bags, for absolutely everything, and I realized I hadn't heard those two words since I had left. "It's free." It tells you an awful lot about this country if you just think about it for a while.

I came back to job-hunt in New York City and found a position with Vogue Pattern Company as a stylist. That means you spend a lot of time choosing the right pattern for the right fabric, then you have the patterned garments made up for fashion shows and send the clothes out on runways in major department stores across the country. I would say most of the mistakes in sewing are made before you start to sew. That is, you must *style* correctly. The fabric *must* be right for the pattern and vice versa. Too many home sewers don't take enough time to study what fabrics make up well in what patterns. They don't go into ready-to-wear to see how clothes are styled. Also, they don't spend enough time in ready-to-wear trying on clothes to see what looks good on them. There are a few rules about styling that will help you to avoid mistakes.

1. A-line designs take hard-surfaced fabrics like linen or gabardine.
2. Gathered or full-skirted designs take soft, fluid fabrics like chiffon or crepe.
3. Don't use large stripes going around the body, as they run downhill, at the side seams.
4. Don't use a big check or plaid in a suit, only in a coat or cape. The plaid of the skirt will never match the plaid of the jacket once you start moving your body. Such a suit is fine on a hanger but not on a body. You can use the plaid in a skirt *under* the coat or cape, however, as the plaids are not moving against each other.
5. Dark colors minimize and light colors maximize, so put dark colors at the hip area and light colors near your face.
6. Bright or pastel colors are needed by women as they get older.
7. A bicolor dress is more interesting than a one-color dress.
8. When making a coat and dress as an ensemble, be sure the design of the coat is repeated in the dress. In other words, if the coat is an A-line or has a drop-shoulder sleeve, then the dress underneath must be an A-line or have a drop-shoulder sleeve.
9. Don't use large flower prints in a tight-fitting dress. They should be used only for large, flowing designs.
10. When combining prints with checks and stripes, be sure they are all of the same size or scale for a pulled-together look.

There are a few other rules too and here they are:

When you have finished making your garment, you're only 60 percent finished. The last 40 percent is the choice of accessories you must make to complement the garment. You've never seen a fashion show where the models were barefoot or without belts, scarves, hats or gloves, have you? Well, that's what fashion is all about: *accessories,* believe it or not. I've seen some doggy garments that looked great once they were accessorized. Why don't American women understand this? They put so much effort into the garment itself and none where it is *really* needed.

A few general rules on accessorizing are:

1. Try to match your shoe to the hem of your garment. Also, it's nice to follow through with a stocking of the same color for a long-line look.
2. In skin-tone stockings, match your stocking to your hand and face color.
3. With a print fabric, match your shoe to the background color.
4. Wear only neutral-color gloves. For example, black, brown, beige, navy, gray.
5. Wear jewelry at only three areas on your body unless you really can carry off the massing on of gold and silver.
6. Don't ever wear a wrist watch with an evening or party dress, please.
7. Don't wear more than three colors at one time (except in the case of prints) and try to count your hair as a color.
8. Do have your coat long enough to cover the top of your boots. The general rule for heel height is: the longer the skirt, the higher the heel.
9. A certain type of hair style demands a certain type of dress.
10. Invest in a full-length mirror. It will become your *best* fashion accessory.

Vogue Pattern had been offered a fashion show from France featuring Boussac fabrics and four Parisian models to travel with it. They had a commentator but she couldn't come during the first month of the tour so I took the four girls and five hundred pounds of luggage and set off. Now these girls didn't speak a word of English so I had to order their food, pay their hotel bill, get doctors and medicine for them and be their go-between with the outside world. I think a group of three-year-olds would have been easier to handle. We started off in Ohio, went down to Philadelphia, out to Saint Louis and then flew back east and landed in Rochester, New York, in a blizzard. We were the last plane to land before they grounded all flights. There was nine feet of snow on the ground and more coming down every minute. We got into our hotel rooms and for the next twenty-four hours it did nothing but snow. I was just thinking we would have a rest there as nobody would come out in that weather for a show when I heard a knock on my door. I opened it and all four models burst into my room with an ultimatum. Either they got to see Niagara Falls or they were taking the first plane back to Paris. When they had signed up for this tour in Paris, they were told they would see America, but all they had seen were hotel rooms, department stores and airports. And they had had enough. I immediately got on the phone to see about renting a car ("Lady, are you out of your mind?"), hiring a cab and driver ("I would give you one but nobody here is crazy enough to do it") or dig up somebody with a car and a lot of nerve who needed money badly. Just at that moment the telephone rang and it was my boss in New York City, inquiring as to how it was going. I told her about the ultimatum and the weather conditions and she thought a moment and then said, "Have you thought about renting a helicopter?" Immediately visualizing our being blown into the falls in one of those things, I realized she was clearly too far away from the situation to understand it, so I hung up and called the university, asking for a student who wanted to make some money driving a car to Niagara Falls. I finally found a girl who was

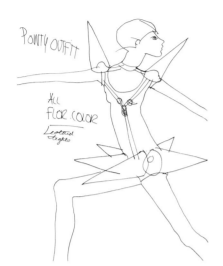

POINTY OUTFIT

ALL
FLOR COLOR

Leotard
tights

Albert "Kayo" Harris

A twenty-first-century space design (left) by Betsy Johnson for the first pattern/fabric psychedelic fashion show.

putting her husband through the seminary and who was desperate enough to drive us. It took us six hours to go ninety miles and when we got there we had to bind ourselves together so we wouldn't be blown over the falls. Of course you couldn't even see them, there was so much snow, but the rebellion was quelled.

When we got to Texas one of the girls met a wealthy Texan who followed us in his own plane. He couldn't speak a word of French and she couldn't speak a word of English, so they would just sit and stare at each other. One day he gave her a pair of emerald earrings and when she came down to dinner that evening she had the earrings on but they were both on one ear. He came over and wanted to know why she was wearing them that way. When I asked her she said, "Tell him I am a big girl and these are much too small for me. That is why I am wearing

both on one ear!" Needless to say, she got a pair of larger earrings.

There are several different kinds of fashion-show tours. Some are lighting shows, for which you take technicians along with you; for some you provide only the clothes, while for others you bring models, clothes, slides and all accessories. My most memorable tour involved two twenty-year-old hippie lighting technicians who had never been west of the Hudson River in New York. This was the heyday of Haight-Ashbury in San Francisco and since our tour ended in that city, that was more than enough reason for these young men to sign up for the tour. Besides, they wanted to see Indians, cowboys and tumbleweeds, and our thirteen-city tour would provide all of that. It would also provide some very square, uptight department store people whom they didn't particularly want to see, but that's another story.

26

The show for this tour turned out to be the breakthrough in this country for models who didn't model but rather danced down the runway. It had been done, successfully, by Mary Quant in London so I thought I couldn't go all that wrong. Besides, there were some very talented people around who could do a lot with a strobe light and the new field of psychedelic lighting. They also came up with some unique, one-of-a-kind ideas. For instance, they designed a dress that had tiny white lights going around the skirt spelling out words (a battery was sewn in the lining). Another dress had musical buttons, that is, each button had a tiny battery under it and when you pressed the buttons, they played do-re-mi-fa-sol-la-ti-do! Sure it was a gimmick, but you don't squash talent. You let it breathe, grow and expand and if some ideas don't work out commercially, that's all right. You owe it to talent to back it and only give direction when absolutely needed. Talent is a rare and beautiful thing in a person, a reason for that person to live freely, that is if others *let* him live and don't force him to conform to their rules. So entered the era of the long-haired, shabbily dressed, sometimes barefooted, pot-smoking hippie which caused my mother to comment to another mother, "Now I know why our daughters aren't married. Look at the people they have to associate with!"

The look that our young technicians got when they boarded a plane was one of complete confusion and more than once they were mistakenly called girls or young ladies. Children followed them on the street because in the towns we visited, nobody had ever seen people who looked or dressed as they did. But they were good at their work. They set up their equipment, handled all the cues for special lighting effects and music and then just as professionally took down the equipment and packed it to go to the next city.

I had toured all these cities before and had friends who took us to dinner, so when we got to San Francisco, where the boys had friends, they invited me along to see Haight-Ashbury. I thought the safest way to see it was probably with a hippie so I went but I definitely cramped their style. I was too properly dressed for them so we went into a bead store and they quickly strung some bright, colorful beads and hung them around my neck so I wouldn't stick out quite so much. Then we went to see their friends. Nobody was really introduced to anybody and everybody was kind of staring off into space. No questions were asked about how we got to San Francisco or what we were doing there and the whole feeling was one of emptiness and sadness. Everybody slept in their clothes on the floor and a stale chocolate cake was dinner for all that evening. It was so depressing to me that when one of them asked me if I would like to go to a "hangar party" that evening, I immediately said yes just to get out of the place. I didn't even question what a hangar party was. After all, California is in the aircraft business and there was probably an old abandoned hangar somewhere. Yessiree, an old abandoned hangar. It didn't dawn on me until we got to the house where the party was being held and I was given a *coat hanger*. When I said I would keep my jacket on, the hippie who brought me said in a disgusted tone of voice, "You don't know what a hanger party is, do you?" I had to admit I didn't, but I got the picture fast so I turned on my heel and walked out. Talk about sad people. They take the cake, a stale chocolate one.

When there is trouble in this country, sometimes the mechanics of just getting from one city to another are almost overwhelming, especially when you are on a tour schedule of a city every two days. I was on a thirty-five-city show tour in the summer of 1968 when the country was undergoing riots and *that* situation was complicated by an air traffic controller's slowdown. Lastly, a rash of summer rainstorms and floods added to the confusion. I was working in Kansas City, Missouri, one day, and had a show to do in Akron, Ohio, the next day. I had to go through Chicago's O'Hare airport, where, at two o'clock in the morning, three thousand of us were stranded due to the slowdown and the storms. Everybody was crabby and snarling at each other until, mixed in with all the announcements of delays, came a voice that sounded like Flip Wilson's, saying, "Here come de judge, Here come de judge." Everybody in the airport broke up and we immediately felt better about our situation.

I got into Akron around 4 A.M., and as the town was under curfew and martial law, I was met by a police escort to get me into the city and my hotel. I passed by U.S. tanks and soldiers silhouetted by burning buildings. It was eerie to see this happening to my country. I got to the store early the next morning and was told that the show had been advertised and would definitely go on though they were afraid of a bomb possibly going off in the auditorium. They asked me if I thought getting a black model or two would help the situation. I couldn't believe their even questioning such a thing under the circumstances, but I nodded and they went to the telephone to start calling. As they had never hired a black model before, they had no list but they finally located a young woman, about thirty, who had never modeled but consented to help out. She had the skinniest legs I have ever seen (I immediately thought: Three cheers for knee-high boots), her face was disfigured on one side due to a large birthmark (thank goodness Garbo-style hats were in) and she had just had an operation for breast cancer and had not yet been fitted with a prosthesis (bulky wool coats cover

anything). I must say that even though she was extremely nervous, she looked terrific in her garments and saved the day. Our audience was small but the store people were pleased that they had been able to stick to their advertised word. I, of course, was never so glad to get out of any town and haven't been back since. It was an awful summer of traveling, and one I would like to forget.

Did you know that you can go from birth to death in paper clothes? That you can be wrapped in a paper bunting at birth and buried in a paper shroud? That is just one of the facts you learn when you do a paper-fashion show. Believe it or not, disposable wear is big business in this country. Most of it is worn by hospital lab technicians, surgeons and the like, but many more areas are utilizing paper and most people are not even aware of it. Both political parties buy enormous amounts of paper clothes, all geared to last only through the intended period of campaigning. There are paper bikinis and, well, as we now have corrugated cardboard paper furniture, I wouldn't be surprised to read about a paper *house* someday!

Paper fashions at least provided some variety among the shows I was producing out of New York City, where I was now in business for myself. One day I was offered a job by the Singer Company (of sewing machine fame) to be their fashion director in New York and I accepted. I felt fashion-showed to death by then and thought the Singer Company would at least give me a chance to do something other than shows. I had a million and one ideas of what could be done in such a job because I had been traveling for many years, working and talking with women, and I had heard more than just a few complaints. My ideas went all the way from making sewing machines in solid bright colors to building sewing wall units in volume for subdivision home contractors. In my opinion, nothing was too small or too big to accomplish. What I wasn't prepared for on my first day of work was to get a call from the president of the company asking me to fly out to Los Angeles to test for teaching sewing on national television—on the Dinah Shore show, no less! A new daytime show called "Dinah's Place" was to be aired in early August and they wanted a sewing expert to appear on the show once a week. Singer had decided it would be a good show for me to appear on and I flew out. I wasn't really nervous, but I sure was curious. What's a celebrity such as Dinah Shore really like? What are Hollywood people—producers, agents—like? I started to find out soon enough because when I arrived I went straight to the studio and met the head man. His name was (and is) Henry Jaffe and he was the person responsible for dreaming up the show, getting Dinah to do it and then getting NBC to buy it. Talk about a mover! No grass has ever grown underneath his feet. He has so many credits for producing and getting on the air such television shows as the "Bell Telephone Hour" and the Chevy show that you wonder how one man could ever accomplish so much. He is an unassuming man, quiet and soft-spoken, but behind his fashionable shades is a pair of eyes that don't miss a thing and a mind that is constantly clicking. We got into his car and drove to the rambling house of Dinah Shore in Beverly Hills. The home décor was very warm and friendly, with lots of needlepoint pillows around that had been made by Dinah herself. She was in the dining area wearing a bright yellow sweater and white pants and was exactly as you see her on television. Inquisitive, interested in what people have to say and very open and friendly. She knows a lot about food and there was a dish of chicken pieces to nibble that she passed around and wanted everyone to try. She is an amazing eater, and can eat enormous amounts of food without gaining weight. One of her friends says that she has the taste of a gourmet and the appetite of a truckdriver; I agree. Through it all, she keeps an incredibly good figure. I have come to the conclusion that she must starve herself in private to eat freely in public! Besides liking food, she has a weakness for beautiful clothes and for tennis, as evidenced by closet upon closet full of clothes and a dream of a tennis court in her backyard. She has a teen-age son named Jody and a daughter, Melissa, who's a strikingly beautiful, dark-haired girl in her mid-twenties.

Dinah's real name is Fanny Rose Shore and she's from Nashville, Tennessee. She started singing in school and church and later graduated to nightclubs and hit records (who can ever forget "Buttons and Bows"?). She would rather sing than do anything else. And in fact, one of the plusses of doing "Dinah's Place" was the song she would sing each day on the show. So, having met her, it was time to work with her. She had a marvelous cotton patchwork wrap skirt that she wore over her exercise leotard and we both thought that would be a good thing to teach how to make on the show.

The studio lot where the show is taped in Hollywood is KTLA; it belonged originally to Paramount Pictures. The buildings are all old and large, made of airy pink stucco. A blue-uniformed guard lets you pass through the front gate, where people line up to get in to watch the TV shows being taped. The people who work on Dinah's show are the friendly sort and the atmosphere on the set is usually a relaxed one. On one side there's a row of dressing rooms for the guests on the show. Your name is put on the door of one of them when you arrive, and you use that dressing room to change clothes, touch up makeup or even take a nap, as each dressing room has a small studio bed in it. At the end of this row of dressing rooms there is a makeup room, where two barber chairs are set up for the makeup people to do their thing on you. Television lights tend to wash color out of your face, so the makeup people put color back in as well as lengthening noses, narrowing cheeks, opening up eyes and a million and one other tricks they have in their kits. They use a lot of makeup and I always thought you look better with it than without it, but apparently the crew on the set don't notice the difference because, checking up on the time left until taping, they often asked me if I had been in makeup yet when I had just spent a whole hour there! Next to the makeup room is a good-size soundproof room known by theatrical tradition as the green room. It has a bar, soft black leather couches and a black-and-red-plaid wall-to-wall carpet. The focal point of the room is a built-in color TV screen where the VIPs watch the show as it is being taped.

On the other side of the set is the kitchen, where the food is prepared for the show, as well as Dinah's dressing rooms. Both places are off limits but then of course some rules are meant to be broken, especially when the air is filled with the smell of a simmering meat sauce, tummies are empty and the last show has just been taped. Dinah Shore has an assistant who gets all the clothes for Dinah to wear on the show, plus her own makeup man and her own hairdresser. They are on the set at all times watching for a shiny nose or a hair out of place. There is also a full-time seamstress, a cook, a prop man, script girls, stagehands, cameramen, light men, sound men, musicians and a director—altogether about forty people.

The set itself is strikingly similar to Dinah's private home. It is built in the round, with a fully equipped kitchen that has an overhead mirror (which is how they get those camera shots looking down on pots cooking away), dinette, living room, den, sewing room and greenhouse. The cameras are in the center and they just swing around the semicircle of rooms to get the shots they want. Thus a variety of backdrops are easily achieved.

On the other side of the set is a group of risers for the audience. Dinah—practically everyone—performs better when there are real, live people watching and clapping, so an audience is brought in for each show. Three shows are taped in a day, the first one at noon, the next around three and the last at six-thirty in the evening. Show times change according to the intricacies of each show but they try to hold to some kind of schedule. Shows are planned according to a theme or to a guest who has been booked. For instance, if it is to be an Indian show, the food, sewing tips, guests and music are all geared to the Indian culture. If Michael Caine or Burt Bacharach are the guests, then the show is positioned around their special areas of talent and hobbies. About a month before you tape a group of shows, you are told who the guests will be on those shows and/or what the themes are. Then you have to plan segments to fit in with each show.

Sometimes it works the other way around, as in the case of Doc Severinsen, a genius with the trumpet who is the musical director of the Johnny Carson "Tonight" show. I knew of Doc's vast wardrobe because his wife, Evonne, is a super home sewer. She's the one responsible for making all those way-out clothes for him and I thought a show with Doc, his clothes and his music would be an entertaining one. So I called Doc, set it up with his agent and the director of "Dinah's Place," and that's how Doc came to be on the show.

A side story here is that Doc brought a dozen or more of his outfits with him and when it came time to tape the show, he looked beautiful in a spangle-laden blue velvet suit, but I didn't have a thing to wear.

We are both about the same height, so I quickly slipped into one of his suede suits and nobody knew the difference. We didn't have time to tell Doc, though, and all through the show he kept staring at me as though he had seen me someplace else but didn't know where. He has so many clothes —about two hundred outfits are made up a year—that he couldn't keep track of them if he tried. Evonne, needless to say, has turned most of the sewing over to someone else. She has enough sewing to do for herself and for their five children.

A lot of funny things happen when shows are being put together. For example, there was the day the Japanese seamstress didn't have the blue velvet slippers ready for me to take to California to tape a show. Pearl Bailey was to be the guest on that show and because she is always complaining about her tired feet, I decided to demonstrate how to make a pair of bedroom slippers. As a special gift for Miss Bailey, I had ordered a pair of pearl-encrusted, mink-lined, blue velvet slippers made up for her. I had called her secretary to get her shoe size, which is rather large, and thought nothing more about it until I got to the home of the Japanese seamstress, who does special sewing projects, and found they weren't ready because I had given her the "wrong size for a lady." I looked at her tiny size-four foot and realized she could never understand or even visualize the foot of Miss Bailey. She hurriedly made them up, however, and the first thing Pearl Bailey said when I gave them to her was, "Are they big enough?" By the way, I read Pearl Bailey's book *Talking to Myself* before the show and wept all the way through it. She has written down a lot of her quiet thoughts and they are extremely moving. Having worked with a number of celebrities and seen what celebrity status can do to a human being, I was especially taken by a small paragraph in which Miss Bailey talks about achieving success and fame late in her life rather than early on. Here it is:

"I'm glad now that I didn't make it when I thought best. Better to make it in God's time than in mine, because now, a little older, a little more mature, I can cope with it, *almost*."

It's not easy being a celebrity. You're not different. It's just that the world treats you differently.

When Leslie Uggams was going to be on the show, I got a call from the director saying Dinah and Leslie were going to wear hot pants (a fad, and that's being kind) on the show and therefore would I wear them? I wasn't especially keen about it but I thought if Dinah and Leslie are going to do it, I will too. When I got out to California, Leslie said to me, "They told me you and Dinah were going to wear hot pants so even though I wasn't for it I thought if you two would, I would too." We put our heads together and realized somebody had maneuvered a fast one on us. Anyway, we all wore hot pants, I demonstrated how to sew them and found out that Leslie Uggams is a fantastic sewer. She had even made the hot pants outfit she wore that day. I don't need to say anything about her singing. We all know how great she is at that.

When Carol Burnett came on the show, she didn't have any idea what she was supposed to do. We told her she was going to make a beef stew in the kitchen and then run over to the sewing room on the other side of the set to cut out and sew a dress, all within one half hour. She looked at Dinah and me as though we were crazy (she doesn't cook or sew) and said, "Do I wear a pair of tennis shoes for this?" She went along with it and kept us laughing with stories about her children. One of them, pointing to the lines in her forehead, had asked, "Mommy, why do you have ditches in your head?" After scolding another child once, Carol had asked her if she had anything to say for herself. Expecting an apology, she was stunned when the child looked up at her through tear-stained eyelids and said, "Mommy, how many teeth do you *really* have?" She is a lovely person and was a good sport about running back and forth so much on the set. She even laughed loudly when Dinah came out wearing a Carol Burnett wig and asked her to sign the "Dinah's Place" guest book at the end of that hectic half hour.

When we first started taping sewing segments, I would write questions for Dinah to ask me and the crew would put them on cue cards for her to read. There were sewing points to be made and this helped to bring them out. After a while we didn't need the cards anymore because Dinah, who is naturally curious about everything, would just ask questions as they popped into her mind. The very first show we taped was on American patchwork and how to sew a patchwork wrap skirt. I explained that patchwork is uniquely American because our foremothers wove their own cloth in the early years of this country and each scrap was so precious that after they had cut out their garments they took the scraps and sewed them together in what are now the famous American patchwork quilts. Next, I showed how the patchwork blocks are sewn together and then step by step made the patchwork wrap skirt on camera. I still receive mail asking how to make up that skirt, so here are the instructions for it.

PATCHWORK WRAP SKIRT

Sew together 6-inch squares of cotton fabric, using a ¼-inch seam allowance. To get the length, measure from your waist to your ankle and then add 1 more row of squares for the hem.

(In order *not* to cut a square in half at the hem, you could make your squares 5 inches, 5½ inches or whatever measures out to fit you correctly lengthwise.)

For the skirt waistband, measure your waist and add 8 inches. (This is a *wrap* skirt.) Cut the waistband 4 inches wide (allowing a ½-inch seam allowance).

To get the fullness for the skirt, make it *2½ times* the length of the entire waistband.

Example: If you have a 25-inch waist, you would add 8 inches, making your wrap-skirt waistband 33 inches long. 2½ × 33 is 82½ inches. Therefore, 82½ inches of 6-inch squares sewn together are needed to make the fullness of the skirt.

Gather skirt with 2 rows of gathering stitches and sew onto the entire waistband, spacing gathers evenly. Turn back 1 row of squares lengthwise for skirt hem edge. Use large hooks and eyes to hold skirt on and in place. You can add a square for a pocket if you so desire.

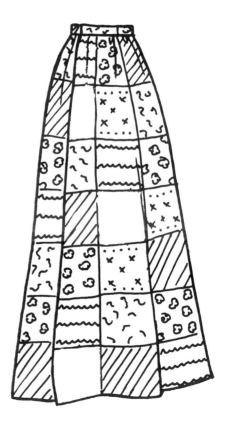

The author with Pearl Bailey and her initialed mink-lined pearl-encrusted blue velvet slippers.

When male guest stars are booked for the show, they are expected to go right along with what is being taught in the areas of cooking, sewing or gardening, as "Dinah's Place" is a service show as well as an entertainment show. Unless you get a Vincent Price, who is a gourmet cook, very few men can add anything in these areas but they certainly can make jokes about what they are given to do. I tried to teach Victor Borge (halfway through, Dinah said, "Francine, why don't you give up?") how to stitch a rya rug. These Scandinavian rugs were originally made to hang on walls in poorly heated homes to help keep the heat in and were later used yarn side down on beds for the same purpose. Now they are made and used as attractive wall hangings or carpets. The stitch is a simple loop of yarn knotted onto a canvas backing but even that was too much for Victor Borge. He ended up by sewing his finger to the canvas, proving that he was really all thumbs . . . or all fingers!

Mike Connors of "Mannix" fame was an-

The author (center) with Dinah Shore and Carol Burnett, who finds that a tongue is a necessary sewing notion when it comes to cutting out a dress.

other male guest star and the sewing spot started off with Mike saying he knew a bit about sewing because he had had to take a course in sewing theater costumes when he was going through drama school at UCLA. He was also on the football team and the windows of the classroom were near the football field. Half the class hour he spent looking for his bobbin on the floor so his football buddies wouldn't see him sitting at a sewing machine. People always ask me about how you adjust a pattern to fit perfectly. So on the day Mike came I had three

models who were all size ten but different heights show how a size-ten pattern needs some alteration for the shortest and tallest. The girls were dressed head to toe in black leotards. I found out that wasn't the thing to teach with Mike Connors. He wanted to help hold the pattern pieces against their bodies but he didn't know where to put his hands. The more he tried, the funnier it got, and very few sewing points were made that day. To help you, the reader, right now, here is the basic way to alter a pattern so that it will fit perfectly:

First, check your measurements against those on the pattern. Lay out the pattern pieces and measure them to be sure that you purchased the correct-size pattern. Then pin the tissue paper pattern pieces together and *try on the pattern.* Note where alterations are to be made. (When you have been sewing for a while you will know even before you try on the pinned-together pattern where the problem fitting areas are going to be.)

Now unpin your pattern pieces. If the pattern was too tight on you, lay the pieces out flat and pick up your scissors with all the courage you can muster. Reason is, you are going to cut some of your pattern pieces in half. Scary, isn't it? You just bought and paid for something and now you are going to shred it all with one snip of the scissors. Not really. It's the only way you can lengthen or widen the pattern to fit you. Go ahead. Cut the pattern pieces apart as is pictured. Next, insert as much plain tissue paper as is needed to alter the pattern to fit you. Lastly, hold it all together with a bunch of pins or some Scotch tape. It's not hard. In fact, it's really easy. Just don't be afraid to do it.

Not everybody is tall and plump; some people are short and skinny. They have an easier time of it because all they have to do is take a *tuck* in their pattern pieces.

Here's another drawing if this is all as clear as mud to you.

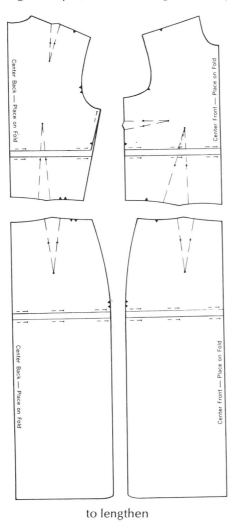

to lengthen

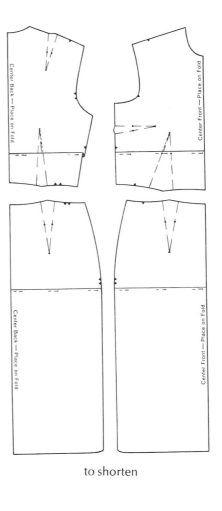

to shorten

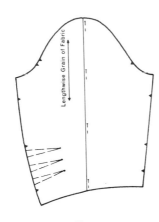

small arms

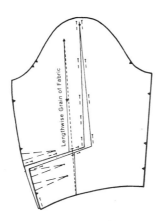

fullness at elbows

After taping a few shows, I learned to type up a list of steps in teaching a subject, memorize it and then go out cold in front of the cameras. This proved to work the best. For instance, here are the *TV steps* for teaching how to make a necktie.

MAKING OF NECKTIE
(5-minute TV spot)

Step 1   Hold up a finished necktie and necktie pattern.
Step 2   Lay fabric out with pattern pinned on.

Step 3   Pin pattern on hair canvas and also on lining.
Step 4   Cut out all pieces of necktie.
Step 5   Sew necktie center seam and sew necktie corners.
Step 6   Trim corners.
Step 7   Press necktie seam open. Then press lining seam allowance down.
Step 8   Turn mitered corners and press.
Step 9   Press seam allowance on one side of tie.
Step 10   Hand-sew lining to necktie, leaving ¼-inch edge.
Step 11   Lay hair canvas interlining in center of tie and gently pin, tucking hair canvas ends under lining.
Step 12   Turn unpressed side to center of necktie and then lap over the other side of the necktie, pinning to secure.
Step 13   Finish with a blind hemming stitch by hand.

When Louie Nye was on, I taught him how to sew on a four-hole suit button so that it doesn't come off. (Put a wooden matchstick between cloth and button and sew the button on. When you've finished, pull out the matchstick and wind thread around the shank, which is the threads just under the button that hold the button away from the suit. This method allows room for buttoning the jacket and also keeps your button from coming off.)

Louis Jourdan, who is even more attractive in person than on the screen, if that is possible, agreed to model a man's fake-fur coat on the show, so I took a trunkful of fake-fur garments out to California with me. By now I was making the cross-country Los Angeles–New York trip every couple of weeks and getting used to the schedule of working eight hours in the Singer office in New York and then catching an evening plane to Los Angeles, which was an even eight-hour trip, door to door. When I checked into the Beverly Hills Hotel it was 1 A.M., my time, and I was usually crabby

Francine teaching Dinah the art of making a necktie. "Bias" is the secret word.

and ready for bed. Nothing is more irritating than to have a hot-shot hotel guest try and pick you up as you register and walk to your room, especially when you are as exhausted as I usually was on arrival. One man I remember tried to start a conversation, using the weather, the hotel guest list and whatever else came to his mind. When he saw he wasn't getting anywhere, he spied the luggage tag on my suitcase and said, "Why, you're from New York. I'm a New Yorker too." I said, "Really? So are eight million other people." Grrr! The

perils of traveling alone!

To get back to more pleasant thoughts, Louis Jourdan was genuinely interested in how fake fur is made and how it is sewn. For all of you home sewers, fake fur is a deep-pile fabric made with synthetic yarn. Often the yardage has pelt markings similar to those of the real fur it represents and these markings should be matched when sewing seams. Cut fake fur so that the pile runs down, just as a furrier treats a real fur. Simple pattern styles with raglan or dolman sleeves are best for deep-pile fabrics. There

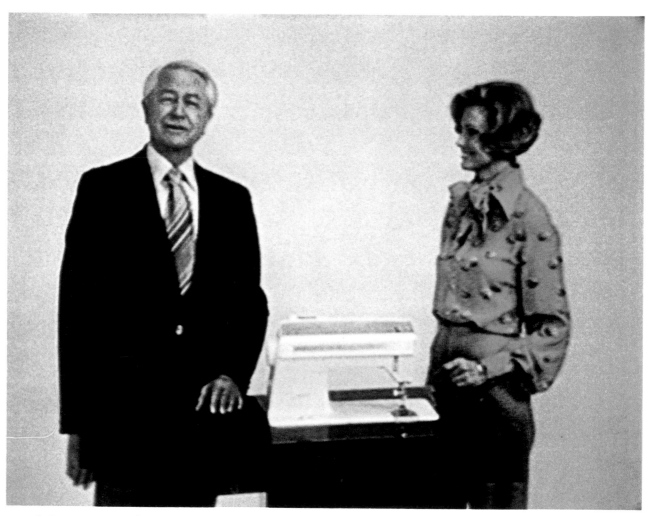

Robert Young and Francine Coffey with the latest member of the Singer family, the Futura sewing machine.

are tricks to sewing it too. For instance, when you are stitching a seam some of the pile will be caught in it. To loosen the pile, work from the right side with a heavy needle, raising the pile covering the seam, as seams in fake fur should never show on the right side. To eliminate bulk from the inside seam allowances, trim off the pile and catch the seam edges to the backing with hand stitches. To prevent facings from rolling, pin them in place from the outside ½ inch from the edge. Turn the facing back and slip-stitch the facing to the garment. Lastly, since but-

tonholes are difficult to make in fake fur, large hooks and eyes or loops are best as fasteners.

Another male guest star was Dennis Weaver, who plays McCloud and was on the long-running western TV show "Gunsmoke." We decided to do a show on recycling clothes and started out with denim jeans, as cowboys have always worn them to protect their legs from sagebrush and cactus. To get extended use out of jeans, worn places can be covered with patches, personalized appliqués, stars, nailheads or whatever you have on hand. Denim is a fabric with a most interesting history. It originated in Nîmes, France, during the Middle Ages and was used by Columbus for the sails of the *Santa María*. Called *serge de Nîmes* (cloth of Nîmes), it was later Americanized to "denim." "Dungarees" comes from the Hindi word *dungri,* for a coarse, inferior Indian calico, and "jeans" got their name from the seaport town of Genoa, Italy, where sailors wore the heavy cloth in pants. Denim has of course outfitted sailors down to this day, but you may be surprised to learn that Henry VIII ordered a shipload of it to outfit the palace staff!

Other items to recycle besides jeans are scarves, which can be made into halters, handbags, blouses or neckties; old fur coats, which can become new fur pillows; and embroidered Indian wall hangings or Victorian patchwork quilts, which you can transform into evening coats and jackets. I even saw a vest made out of five hundred rubber bands that had been crocheted together, with different color rubber bands for the border. All you had to do was stretch it over your head to put it on and I must say it showed up beautifully on a black leotard top. Lastly, what about old neckties? They make a marvelous evening skirt. I know because I have one. Here's the way you do it.

NECKTIE SKIRT

Select old ties of approximately the same width and shade. The bright colors and bold prints of the newer ties will take away from the beauty of the more subdued colors of the old ties. Do *not* mix fabrics. Select all cotton, all wool, all wool-knit or all polyester-knit ties.

Not all ties are the same length. Be certain that the narrow ends are of equal length. You may have to shorten them in preparing the overskirt. The narrow-end overskirt should be about 8 inches shorter than the wide-end underskirt.

Open the backs and remove the linings. Mea-sure from waist to knee and add 5/8 inch for seam allowance at the waist. Cut each tie this length, saving the narrow ends for the overskirt. Sew each piece together where the fold was and trim off excess fabric. Measure around your waist and add 8 to 10 inches more in ties to allow for gathering. Make the overskirt with the narrow ends and baste the waistband to the two pieces of fabric. Attach waistband so that you have a casing for elastic. The elastic should be cut the same length as your waist plus an inch for stitching the ends together. Run elastic through casing and stitch. You can finish the pointed hem by top-stitching the points or hemming by hand.

The day we had Rob Reiner of "All in the Family" on, the making of a man's shirt was the lesson. At Singer we had found out in our sewing classes for men that there were certain differences in teaching men and women how to sew. Men had trouble picking up a straight pin due to the large size of their fingers, so we started using pins with brightly colored ball heads to make it easier for them. Also, the cutting scissors were not comfortable. Men's thumbs are so much larger that they were picking the scissors up backward and then wondering why they weren't cutting well. We got larger-size scissors. Almost every man wanted to start out by sewing a shirt for himself. The easiest shirt pattern possible was found, with no inset neckband or buttons, and the men were able to handle it as a first project. Here it is:

Sometimes I have an idea to try something unusual and it works out so well that it surprises even me. I had long been thinking of making up a jeweled evening ensemble out of plain old red bandannas. Designwise, I envisioned a short cropped quilted jacket over a white satin shirt with a long gathered skirt, and all glittering with a thousand and one jewels. Impossible, you say. Never, if you know how to sew. Some of the best garments came out of a vague dream or two of mine and you know it's a success when Oscar de la Renta, the famous Seventh Avenue designer, keeps staring at you and finally comes up and asks, "Who designed your garment?"

So off to the dime store to buy red bandannas, three for a dollar. Then, sewing them together, quilting them, making up the garment and lastly jeweling it. All I can say is, Dinah Shore took one look at the finished product and immediately wanted to wear it on the show. I had used navy-blue bandannas for the sash and jacket lining. With Dinah's own sparkle and the sparkle of all those glittering jewels, it was something to see. Here's a sketch and the instructions. Dream a little bit and I'm sure you'll see just how great it can look on you.

RED QUILTED BANDANNA EVENING ENSEMBLE

Pattern

There is no one pattern. Any basic long gathered skirt and Chanel-type jacket will do. The jacket should be shortened to give it the bolero look.

Bandannas and notions

The bandannas may be purchased in men's clothing stores, dime stores or army/navy surplus stores. The cost is about three bandannas for a dollar. Approximately twenty-two bandannas will be needed for a size 10 outfit. Eight blue bandannas should also be bought for the jacket lining and sash. Cotton batting will be needed to back the bandannas when quilted.

Rhinestones

Buy glass rhinestones the size of a dime with two small holes in them so that they may be hand-stitched to the bandanna jacket and skirt.

Quilting

If you live in or near a large city, you can have a piece of fabric quilted for a very small charge. If this is not possible, you can quilt the fabric yourself by using the quilting attachment. Before quilting, examine a piece of machine quilting carefully to learn how far apart the quilting lines are made. Use a rather large stitch when quilting.

Note

Many of the bandannas manufactured around the country are not colorfast. Dry cleaning is essential for your garment.

Sewing, quilting, and cutting

Sew the red bandannas together three across to form a length of yardage. Quilt the bandannas. Cut out and sew the jacket and skirt. Sew the blue bandannas together. Do *not* quilt this. Just cut the jacket lining out of it and a 3-inch-wide fold-over sash cut on the bias to go around the waist and tie in a knot. Make up a shirt or sleeveless turtleneck blouse in pure white satin. Lastly, spend many a pleasant hour sewing the giant rhinestones on the skirt and jacket in any decorative pattern you like. It's a winner of a garment!

If after you've read this you are weary at the mere prospect of all the work involved, you'll be happy to know there are other ways to use bandannas. Just sewn together they make a marvelous tablecloth. Use red for the cloth and blue for the napkins. Or with a bit more work, make up denim place mats. Bind off the edges with red bias tape and use a red bandanna as a napkin. Add a blue jeans pocket to hold the silverware and a Levi Strauss leather patch for a water glass coaster. It's easy and here's how you do it.

DENIM PLACE MAT

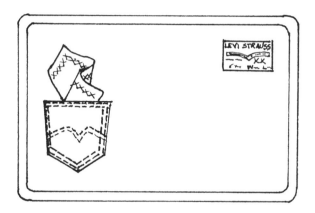

Cut a place mat of navy-blue denim measuring 18 inches by 12 inches. Round off the corners and bind all the way around with 1-inch-wide red bias tape. Fold over the bias tape and hand-stitch on the back. You can also top-stitch to hold it down. When finished, the edge should appear ½ inch wide on top of mat. For added stiffness, you can back this place mat with a layer of press-on Pellon.

To make a coaster for a water glass, take a leather patch from a pair of Levi Strauss blue jeans and top-stitch it (in red thread) to the upper-right-hand corner of the mat.

For a napkin holder, cut out pocket shape according to a jeans pocket, adding ½ inch to turn under. Top-stitch a double row of red stitching as is pictured and *then* turn under ½-inch edge and *hand-stitch* pocket to place mat in lower-left-

43

hand corner. Remember to leave top of pocket open in order to insert a red bandanna to use as a napkin.

One of the loveliest stars I met and worked with on the show was Kay Starr. Her "Wheel of Fortune" recording was number one on the "Hit Parade" for months when I was growing up and she sings that song as well today as she did back in the fifties. She is part Indian and has done more than just about any other private citizen to help educate Indians. I had some Indian skirts that were so exquisite in workmanship that they were well worth showing on national TV. They had been given to me by a young Indian woman who had come to Singer to request more sewing machines for her reservation. For years Singer has had a program of giving away machines to groups such as the Mountain Artisans of West Virginia or any of the Indian tribes. So I immediately put my hand on the phone to order them. She had asked for fifty machines, which was no problem, but her next request stopped me cold. She wanted them all to be the old treadle model! Seems that some reservations were without electricity and they were the only machines that could be used. Believe me, it's a lot easier to get fifty new machines from the factory than to round up fifty of the treadle model, but it was done. To get back to the skirts, they were made of very bright and colorful cotton strips, miniature pieces of cotton patchwork and miles and miles of baby rickrack. I have never seen anything that has as much work on it as those skirts. I would not counsel anybody to make one but if you are a glutton for punishment, *do* use a rickrack attachment. It might keep you from talking to yourself! As every skirt is different, there is no pattern but here is a sketch if you are inclined to make one.

When Della Reese came on the show she brought her daughter Dumpsey, a shy, lovely eleven-year-old. I decided to show how to make a bedroom for a young lady and I did it all in blue-and-white gingham checks. I started with the windows, doing something so easy that I'm almost embarrassed to tell you what it is. The curtain was one length of gingham that was nothing more than poufs of fabric gathered and held in place by bows. Here's how you do it.

1. Measure width of window. Fabric on each side should measure 1½ times the window width. Finished length of fabric should be double the window length.
2. Divide each fabric length into 3 equal parts. Sew ribbon and rod casings as pictured.
3. Thread with narrow ribbon, gather and tie.
4. Attach cup hooks to window frame at desired intervals. Hang ribbon on hooks.
5. Finish with ribbon bows and valance.

44

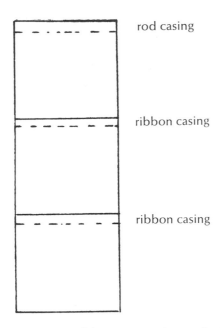

rod casing

ribbon casing

ribbon casing

Then I showed how to make a gingham pillow sham, a bedspread with a dust ruffle (I sew my dust ruffle onto an old bed sheet and safety-pin it to the box springs to keep it from slipping) and a round tablecloth (directions for making one are in the Christmas booth toward the back of this book). That was all I had time to teach on the show that day but I certainly don't believe in stopping there. The brightest and most imaginative way to give a room a new look is with fabric and a sewing machine. (Paint might be quicker but it is also messier!) When you choose fabrics for your home you add your own personal warmth, which no one can duplicate. Start out by covering the walls of your room with fabric. Amazing how all the

cracks in the plaster are a thing of the past once you do! Here are the steps for doing it.

1. Measure walls for yardage required.
2. Cut and seam fabric lengths for one wall at a time.
3. Tack 1-inch-wide strips of ¼-inch wood beneath ceiling or upper moldings, just above floor moldings, and vertically at corners.
4. Working with another person, begin tacking fabric with a staple gun to wood strips at ceiling. Pull fabric taut and staple to bottom wood strips. Staple fabric at corners.
5. Finish edges and corners by gluing self-covered cording to cover staples. See how easy it is and how great it looks!

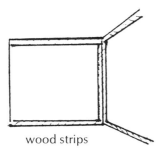

wood strips

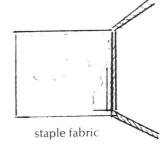

staple fabric

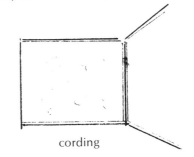

cording

The author (center) showing Joan Rivers and Dinah Shore how to make the "people skirt"...

A historical note is that fabric on walls has been used through the centuries, mostly for warmth but also as a decorative device. The most elegant walls were first padded with a soft flannel before being covered with fabric. This gave the fine jacquards and brocades that were used a certain body and richness.

If you like what you've done so far, you can also fabric your ceiling, or if you really feel adventurous, why not *fabric a floor?*

After choosing your design, glue the fabric down with Elmer's Glue or Sobo diluted slightly with water. You can make a tile effect or even a patchwork design by butting the fabric edges together. (Use cotton fabric heavy enough so the glue doesn't show through and a sharp razor blade to get clean edges.) After you are completely paralyzed from laying your fabric floor and convinced you will never walk upright again, cover, via a paintbrush, with several layers of polyure-

46

...and talking with Jayne Meadows and Dinah Shore about a unique idea called Cut 'n' Sew.

thane coating, being sure the glue is dry before you do so. For a really hard finish, use up to eight coats. (You should plan to stay with friends during this process, for the odor of polyurethane is most unpleasant while it is drying; however, it vanishes quickly once it is completely dry.)

One show that I will never forget featured Joan Rivers. I had seen her on a TV talk show and she had been wearing what I termed the "people skirt." It was a long skirt entirely made of sequins that pretty much told the story of her life. ("A lot of mistakes!" as she said later on "Dinah's Place.") There were the dates of her wedding and of the birth of her daughter, Melissa, pictures of her home and many personal things about her life. The sequins were of different colors and sewn on chiffon so that the skirt was light-looking and fell softly around her body. Well, the last show of the year was coming up and I wanted to do something special for Dinah. When I was told that Joan Rivers would be the guest, I remembered about Joan's "people skirt" and decided to make one for Dinah. Only, instead of her personal life, it

47

would be everything that had happened on "Dinah's Place" during the past year. The skirt was made of navy brushed denim with a red felt border. All the appliqués were in colored felt. There was a flowerpot with the name "Jerry" under it for Jerry Baker, the gardener on the show, and an envelope with the name "Bessie," for Dinah's sister, who handles all the fan mail. The full-length skirt had two dozen appliqués on it and some were inside jokes, such as the title of a song that Dinah had had trouble singing, and a stopwatch because we seldom finished shows on time. The skirt also had a hundred or more giant silver sequins sewed on it so that it sparkled plenty when it was worn. Dinah knew nothing about it and we started taping the show with Joan Rivers making a potholder. When Joan botched that up enough (as only a comedienne can do) I brought out the "people skirt," much to the surprise and delight of Dinah. She shrieked and oohed and aahed over each appliqué and was completely thrilled with it. The skirt was a totally personal thing, something you couldn't go into a store and buy, and maybe that's why I think sewing is so great.

One time Dinah and I did a show on all the different things a sewing machine can do. As I proceeded to the basting, darning, hemming, appliquéing, finishing and sewing stitches, then through all the decorative stitches down to how a sewing machine can even sew on buttons, her eyes grew bigger and bigger until finally she said in a weak voice, "Can it *sing* too?" Dinah has the talent for listening and wanting to learn, which made that lesson especially easy to teach.

Besides "show and tell" shows, we also did "how to" shows, in which I taught how to sew on jewels (a friend of mine uses dental floss), how to match plaids (the even-feed foot is the *only* way), how to press a garment properly (with brown paper, a press cloth, and with a light touch, please), how to

put in hems (a rolled edge is *all* that's allowed) and many more. There were two shows that received the greatest amount of mail. One featured Jayne Meadows and a new idea called Cut 'n' Sew. It was a three-yard length of fabric with items such as potholders, toaster and blender covers, aprons, etc., and the instructions on how to make these items all printed right on the fabric so that literally all one had to do was cut and sew! The other show taught how to sew knits and since that seems to be everybody's bag these days, here are some of my own tips.

1. Wash all knit fabrics before cutting to remove any excess finishing chemicals. This helps prevent skipped stitches and generally makes the fabric easier to sew.
2. To avoid stretching the knit when pinning your pattern, lay it on a large, flat surface. Do not allow the fabric to hang over the edge as this extra weight will stretch the fabric.
3. Because a knit may have a slight nap or texture, be sure to lay out the pattern on your fabric with all pieces facing in the same direction.
4. Nylon zippers are most flexible and best for knits. To prevent puckering later, shrink zippers by soaking in hot water for a few minutes, air drying and pressing lightly.
5. Polyester thread has more stretch strength than cotton thread and should be used for knits.
6. Use one of the new ballpoint sewing machine needles. They push aside, rather than pierce, the yarns of a knit.
7. For sewing a knit, set the stitch length at 12 to 15. Use a narrow zigzag stitch or the stretch stitch available on the newest machines. Use a loose and balanced tension.
8. Most knits do not need to be lined. But if you prefer to use a lining, choose one that will stretch with the outer fabric. Construct the lining separately in dresses,

attaching it only at the neckline and arm-holes.

9. Some sections of the garment should not stretch. Waistline and shoulder seams should be stabilized with seam binding. Sew the tape on as the seam is stitched.

10. To keep edges on lightweight jerseys from curling, use a zigzag or straight stitch ¼ inch from the edge.

11. Nylon stretch lace is perfect for easing in the hem of an A-line skirt. Remember to stretch the lace slightly as you sew it to the hem edge.

12. For a hem that will look great on the inside and outside, place a row of blind hemming stitches at the half hem width from the finished edge. This eliminates some of the fabric weight on the single row of blind hemming stitches that you place ¼ inch from the hem edge. The finished hem should then be lightly pressed for a rolled (but not creased) edge.

13. Pressing as you go along is an absolute must for a perfectly finished garment. Place strips of brown paper under seam allowances as you press. This will prevent ridges on the outside of the garment.

14. Decorative top stitching is a great way to emphasize the design lines of a knit garment. To prevent the fabric from stretching, hand-baste ¼ inch on either side of the line to be top stitched. Use a size 16 needle, 6 to 8 stitches per inch, and a loose tension. Buttonhole twist should be used in the machine needle and regular thread in the bobbin.

Besides working with celebrities on the Dinah Shore show in California, I was working with them in New York. One day I got a call from the Barbara Walters show, "Not for Women Only," asking me if I would come on the program and teach how to cut out and sew a dress. Barbara Walters was doing a week of programs on how to save money and one whole half-hour show was devoted to sewing. This time I didn't have to fly three thousand miles to tape a show. I just took an elevator down fifty-five floors, as NBC and Singer are in the same building in the Rockefeller Center complex of buildings in New York. It was a lovely way to tape a show, I can tell you.

I walked on the set and talked with the prop man about where to set up the cutting board and sewing machine. Five minutes later Barbara Walters appeared, looking lovely in a pink knit sheath dress that had been made up for her from a Vogue pattern. It was the dress we were going to make on camera that day. Without an introduction, explanation or run-through (I had never met her before), the cameras started to roll tape and we were doing the show. She introduced me from a three-by-five card she had in her hand and then we broke for a sixty-second commercial. In that sixty seconds she turned to me and said, "Now, exactly what are we doing?" I answered, "Follow me. We're going from the cutting board to the sewing machine to the accessory sketches and we are making the dress you're wearing." That was it. The cameras started to roll and we did the show straight through. The minute the show was over, the set was cleared and fifteen minutes later another show began. A whole week of half-hour shows are taped in about five hours, and that includes a break for lunch! It was truly the fastest and the most professional thing I had ever seen. Not only that, the show turned out good enough to become a rerun.

Another celebrity whom I have met in New York is Celeste Holm. She had just won the Golden Needle award given by the American Home Sewing Council for her contribution to sewing. We started talking and she said she too had been taught how to sew by her mother. Her most memorable dress was one she made when she was eighteen to wear on a date with John Fitzgerald Kennedy, then a student at Harvard. Need-

Francine teaching Barbara Walters how to make the dress Barbara is wearing on "Not for Women Only."

ing it in a hurry, she rushed to Filene's in Boston and bought a maroon piqué print fabric that had "huge white flowers all over it." The dress she made was long and had tucks going around the bodice, with a white piqué cuff on the strapless top. It was her most successful evening gown. When I met her, she had just finished filming *Tom Sawyer,* and I was delighted when she brought out an evening vest that she had crocheted during her spare time on the set. It was made entirely of gold metallic elastic thread that she then interwove with multicolored ribbons. Talk about one of a kind! But then that's what sewing *can* be all about.

Still another celebrity is Edith Head, the dynamic, dark-haired costume-designing genius of the movie industry who has a grand total of seven Oscars among her awards. We were both guest speakers for a Career Day Seminar in San Francisco and afterward we shared a ride to the airport. I had met Edith before, but now that I was writing a book and had her captive in a car for an hour or so I decided to get some of her interesting stories on paper. I knew she had the world's largest collection of miniature sewing machines, so you can imagine how surprised I was when she said, "This may shock you, but I don't sew. I'm a de-

50

signer who has never learned to sew. Oh, I can do up a hem or put in a sleeve if I have to, but nothing more than that. It's because sewing is a working craft in my business and that's all unionized. I'm not *allowed* to sew!''

And then she reminisced about the first star she ever dressed. It was Mae West in *She Done Him Wrong,* with Cary Grant. "I had just met Mae when she called and asked me to help her pick out a dress for a dinner she was going to. I got to her house, which was all done in white, and found a dozen or so white evening gowns Mae had bought. She finally chose one and then said, 'Now if you lower the hem in front, leave it alone in back and reset the sleeves, I think I can wear it.' I did a basting job with safety pins on the sleeves, which didn't show because she wore a white fur boa, and, well, I, who didn't sew, got that dress together in three hours for Mae West to wear that night!'' I queried, "But if you don't sew, how did you ever get started collecting old sewing machines?'' "I had nothing to do with it,'' she answered. "I had a very elegant French couture salon, which I thought was very chic, but one day Barbara Stanwyck came in and said, 'This place looks more like a boudoir than a salon. I'll send over an old sewing machine to give it the right look.' And she did. Since then, people have sent them to me and I've collected old machines wherever I've been making movies. Last week, I found one in Norway working on the new Jane Fonda film and not too long ago Bette Davis sent me a machine that belonged to her grandmother, which Bette found in the attic. Amazing how the collection has grown. It now numbers over a hundred.''

I of course wondered how she got stars to wear what she designed. She said she uses a bit of applied psychology, which she calls the "give in to the actress/actor syndrome."

She doesn't ever show the star just one sketch with one swatch of fabric. Rather, she shows three sketches with three swatches of fabric and says, " 'Now, which of these do you want to wear?' I let them make the choice so they can't complain later on. It always works and I'm off the hook. Of course, all stars think they have tiny waists and they want the waistline fitted very tightly, which as you know only *shows up* figure faults rather than hides them. So, for the fitting, I do it the way they want and then let it out for the day of shooting. I always comment on how they must have lost weight, which they are happy to hear. I also have my 'one finger' policy with my fitters. One finger held up''—she demonstrated and it looked very natural as she was talking —"means 'Don't pay any attention to the star' and two fingers mean 'Fit it the way she wants it.' It sure saves a lot of problems.

"I always have my first-aid sewing crew on the set. You can't hold up production if a hem comes out. You just get the job done right there. And I always travel with a first-aid sewing kit. By the way, if we're doing an action film, we always double-sew everything, hems, buttons, buttonholes, the whole works. Can't afford to have a sleeve rip out when a star is taking a leap over a fence. Of course for all those Ginger Rogers–Fred Astaire films we made muslins of those gowns to find out if they could dance with all that fabric around their legs. They could and did.'' Unfortunately we arrived at the airport and that ended the interview. One thing I'm sure about. Just the stories of Edith Head could fill a whole book!

Besides celebrities, there are a number of other ways to promote sewing, such as TV commercials, magazine ads, teen-age sewing contests, charity balls (socialites wearing pattern-fabric ball gowns), window displays, newsletters, brochures, sewing demonstrations and, of course, the time-tested fashion

Sewing Wall Unit contains fabric and pattern storage bins, notions drawers, drop-down ironing board, bulletin board, bookcase, and a sewing machine set into a movable parsons table. The unit has a coordinating wardrobe complete with drawers, shelves, and hanging rods.

in any company that's not an easy one. Simply stated, it doesn't turn out a P&L (profit and loss) statement at the end of each quarter and therefore you can't gauge its worth. It is there mainly to counsel departments on how to achieve a fashion image (even if it's only a card to hold a sewing gadget), to do special projects, such as design sewing wall units, or to handle and stage fashion promotions. These can be big or small, going all the way from a national bicentennial promotion to a single in-store demonstration.

Naturally I am always looking for ways to get people into sewing. I've found that I'm not alone either, as I receive a lot of mail asking for ways to turn on (used in the positive sense, please) a Girl Scout troop or group of teen-agers to sewing. I also get mail from people who run church bazaars or charity events asking for ideas in order to make money for their organization. So for all of them and for you, the following pages

54

contain 100 ideas that are tailor made to earn money for a favorite charity or to win newcomers to the world of sewing.

By the way, I have been to many charity bazaars but I have never been very impressed with them. Therefore, before actually setting out to find 100 easy-to-sew easy-to-sell ideas, I decided to research just exactly what church groups, county fairs, women's exchanges and ecology groups were doing at their bazaars. Do you know what I found? They had some great items to sell but they didn't know how to merchandise them. Gadzooks! They never took How to Sell 101. Therefore I am letting you in on an absolute law in the selling business. *It doesn't matter what the product is. You must merchandise it well in order for it to sell.* What's merchandising, you ask? It's how products are *presented* to the buyer. It's amazing to me that people don't understand this. All you have to do is go into a department store and see how *all* products are merchandised in booths, corners or areas with themes and overall color coordination. If you are going to be successful in the bazaar business, you must divide all items into *color* and *people* groups. By that I mean all items for father and grandpa *must* be in one booth and *must* be color coordinated. Nothing looks worse than a mishmash of colors and items. Believe me, you've got to make it look appetizing. In fact, that's really what selling is all about. So now that we've gone this far, here are a few tips on how to put together and stage a successful bazaar.

1. Get together a group of the "doers" in your organization. (Not the ones who *say* they will make so many of one item; the ones you can count on to *make* so many of one item.)

2. Decide how much money you want to raise as a group. Also when and where you want to hold the bazaar. Assign somebody the task of getting a place and then following through on getting the doors unlocked, lights turned on, etc.

3. Go through the suggested 100 items in this book and let your volunteer workers choose the items each wants to make. Note I said "items" with an *s*. This is a serious business and you only want worker bees.

4. For those who can't handle a needle or are afraid of anything mechanical like a sewing machine, don't let them get away. They may not know it yet but they are your cookie and cake bakers, your printing, gluing and cutting experts.

5. Decide on the pricing of each item. I would suggest anywhere from thirty-five cents to five dollars for any item in this book, but then you all know "what the traffic will bear" price-wise in your area better than I so that is really up to you.

6. If you can get fabric and trims donated, so much the better. As an enticement, promise a handwritten tag on each item telling who donated the fabric. Most groups have money in their treasury for the absolute necessities of staging a bazaar, but the rule is: Always try to get things donated first—from shops, stores, anywhere! Of course, need I say, have everybody scrounge for goodies in their scrap boxes at home.

7. To get a steam of enthusiasm up among your volunteers, have a meeting one week after you decide who will make what. Everyone is to bring in her first sample item for plenty of oohs and aahs and compliments all around.

8. Decide on the age and sex that you most want to sell to and then gear your items to them. Next, decide on the number of booths and the colors of each booth. There are four suggested booths in this book, and all four have definite colors. (Am I beginning to sound like a broken record?)

9. Get a couple of teen-age sons who survived Woodworking 102 or some willing

husbands who are new to this kind of thing (you'll have a lot more luck in getting them to do it if they haven't done it before and don't know what's involved) to build the booths (pictured below) for the bazaar. If this is not within the realm of reality, long tables can be used to sell the items. Remember, though, each of the tables has only *one kind* of item on it, either for men, for women or for children, or a Christmas table where the items can be for anybody . . . but hear ye! hear ye! the colors on each table *must* all coordinate!

10. Get posters made announcing the bazaar and put them in store windows. Call up schools and other organizations and have them post the date and time of the bazaar on their bulletin boards. Call up radio stations and get them to make on-the-air announcements.

These are the basic steps in putting together a bazaar. It takes a lot of work but it's amazing how you can get a group or a whole community to pull together when there is a common goal and when they know everybody is doing their share of the work. Bazaars are fun and they can be very profitable so . . . happy sewing and selling!

part two 100 projects to *sew for yourself or a charity bazaar*

ladies' booth

The following ideas are for ladies of *any* age. There are gifts for grandmother to buy for granddaughter, mother to buy for daughter, daughter to buy for mother, or niece to buy for aunt. The colors suggested for all the items in this booth are pink, green and white simply because they are so fresh and feminine. We've mixed checks with prints and prints with solids but, color-wise, "it all hangs together," as they say.

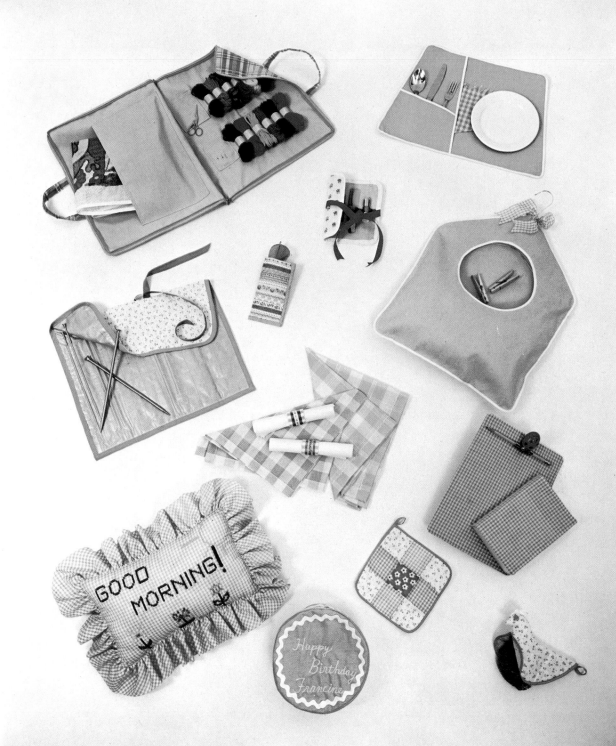

1. good morning/good night pillow

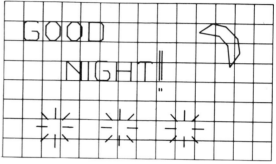

box = 1 sq. in.

A best seller could be a simple-to-make pillow of tiny gingham checks with "Good Morning" on one side and "Good Night" on the other. Words are stenciled on, all ready to be cross-stitched by the customer herself!

Materials

1. ¾ yard tiny gingham check
2. Dressmaker pencil
3. Cotton or polyester fiber stuffing
4. Six-strand embroidery floss

How to

1. Cut two pieces of gingham 10 inches by 14 inches.
2. Cut strip for ruffle on the bias, 7 inches by 96 inches (may be pieced).
3. Following diagram for stencil, put X's on each gingham piece, using "Good Morning" on one piece and "Good Night" on the other.
4. Stitch short ends in ruffle to form complete circle.
5. Fold ruffle strip in half lengthwise, right sides *outside,* and make two rows of gathers along raw edge.
6. Fit and stitch ruffle to all sides of one gingham piece.
7. Pin other side of pillow onto this with right sides together. Stitch on all sides, leaving a 7-inch opening.
8. Turn pillow.

Note: For selling, include a skein of embroidery floss, stuffing and instructions to close 7-inch opening after pillow is embroidered and stuffed by the customer.

2. flowerpot wall caddy

There's nothing like a "place for everything and everything in its place." That's exactly what this charming wall caddy will help do. A design where the tops of the flowerpots are open so that each pot is actually a pocket to hold keys, labels, pencils or even a note pad!

Materials

1. One piece of canvas or burlap 25 inches by 13 inches
2. Felt and gingham scraps of varied colors, large enough to cut out design
3. One 12-inch ruler
4. Two yarn tassels and a 15-inch-long yarn cord

How to

1. Enlarge diagram and cut out flower-pot design in different colors of felt and gingham. Cut flowerpots double, however, placing bottom of rim edge *on the fold*. Then fold over this edge to make the rim. Do not turn under or hem sides and bottoms of pots.
2. Hem canvas or burlap edges by turning under ¼ inch and top-stitching down.
3. Glue felt flowers in place on canvas or burlap and then appliqué around the edges with a zigzag sewing machine stitch.
4. Place small pot on first. Do not glue. Simply use tight zigzag stitch around edges, leaving top of pot open. Do the same with the medium- and large-size pots, overlapping them, consulting Flowerpot Wall Caddy sketch as you go along.

5. Turn down top edge of the caddy and make a 1¾-inch casing. Insert ruler. Attach a 15-inch-long cord at ruler end with two tassels for hanging.

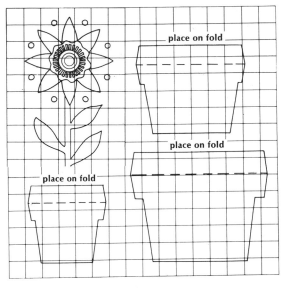

box = 1 sq. in.

63

3. knitting needle case

This is a delightful case to keep knitting needles organized. I've heard that knitters swear by it!

Materials

1. ½ yard small-floral-print quilted fabric (makes two cases)
2. ½ yard solid-color fabric for lining
3. 2 yards ½-inch-wide double-fold bias tape
4. 1 yard of ½-inch-wide grosgrain ribbon to match bias tape
5. Two snaps

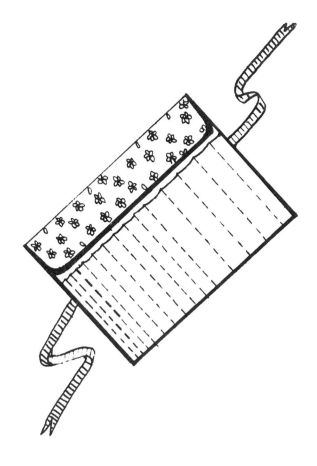

How to

1. Cut one piece of quilting fabric and one piece of lining fabric 19 inches by 16½ inches. Cut another piece of lining fabric 12½ inches by 16½ inches. On shorter lining piece, machine-stitch 1-inch hem along top lengthwise edge.
2. Place shorter lining piece over larger lining piece, matching bottom and sides. Be sure hemmed edge is on top. Do multiple rows of vertical machine stitching ⅝ inch or ½ inch apart to form pockets for needles.
3. Complete case by placing the lining fabric over the quilted fabric, putting wrong sides together. Encase all edges with bias tape. Round the top corners slightly.
4. Fold the top down about 6 inches and sew a snap about 1 inch from this fold at both ends of the case to hold the top down, protecting the needles and keeping them from slipping out.
5. Take a 32-inch-long strip of ribbon. Sew center of this to one edge of the case. Roll the case up and tie ends in a bow.

4. basket sewing box

If you can locate these colorful baskets with handles, they make dandy sewing boxes. A Japanese import store in New York City called Azuma has them. Inexpensive gift shops might house them too.

Materials

1. One basket with handle
2. ½ yard small-checked gingham
3. Cording or ribbon for a drawstring
4. Pincushion

How to

1. Cut a circle of gingham the size of bottom of basket.

2. Cut a piece of gingham the length of the circumference of the circle and the height of the basket plus 5 inches.

3. Sew the short ends of the gingham together, making a narrow French seam.

4. Turn down the top edge ¼ inch and then 1 inch. Stitch, forming a casing, leaving 1-inch opening to pass ribbon or cording through.

5. With right sides together, sew this piece to circle, using a ¼-inch seam allowance.

6. Slip ribbon through casing, leaving two ends long enough for ties.

7. Tack pincushion to side of basket.

8. Place drawstring bag with wrong side out in basket, gluing it to sides and bottom of basket.

9. Fill with sewing notions and tie ribbon ends in a bow to close.

5. sliding clothespin bag or dirty laundry bag

A clothespin bag to slide along the wash line. A bright, pretty way to solve an old washday problem; or use as an attractive laundry bag for soiled lingerie.

Materials

1. Oilcloth or vinyl fabric remnants in bright solids or pastel gingham checks. You need two pieces 16 inches by 20 inches
2. Contrasting double-fold bias tape
3. Wire coat hanger
4. Ribbon

How to

1. Enlarge diagram and cut out pattern.
2. Four inches from top of one piece, draw a circle about 8 inches in diameter. (Use a paper plate as a guide.) Cut out circle.
3. Bind this circle with bias tape.
4. With right sides together, cut fabric at top on angles to match hanger.
5. Round off all corners by cutting them slightly.
6. Using a ¼-inch seam allowance, sew all edges together, leaving a small opening on top for hanger. Bind all around with bias tape. Insert hanger. Lastly, attach a pretty ribbon bow.

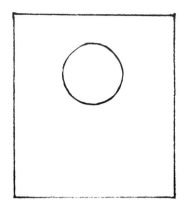

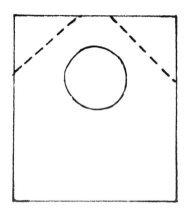

6. office desk place mat

Here's an idea for a place mat—this one has pockets to hold napkin and plastic utensils in place. Great for secretaries when they want to eat lunch at their desk.

Materials

1. ½ yard canvas
2. 2½ yards bias tape
3. ½ yard gingham

How to: Place mat

1. Cut fabric in shapes shown, enlarging the diagram and cutting out the pattern.
2. Sew bias tape along pocket A as shown.
3. Stitch pocket A to B.
4. Sew bias tape along edge of B as shown.
5. Stitch entire pocket unit onto place mat C.
6. Sew bias tape to outer edge, curving corners.

How to: Napkin

1. Cut a 10-inch square of gingham.
2. Machine-stitch 1 inch from edge on all sides, using size 20 straight stitch or a narrow zigzag stitch.
3. Fringe to stitching.

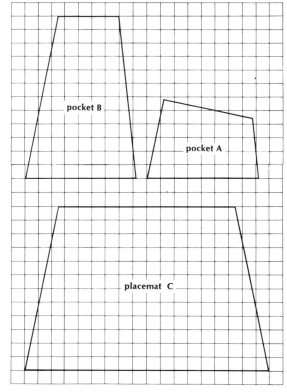

pocket B

pocket A

placemat C

box = 1 sq. in.

67

9. ribbon eyeglass case

A feminine little stocking stuffer or thoughtful remembrance—an eyeglass case of appliquéd ribbon. It is also simple sewing! A careful selection of pretty ribbons (laces and rickrack could be used) ensures a quick-selling item.

Materials

1. Gingham, silk, taffeta, floral cotton: any fabric you feel is suitable for the eyeglass case
2. Lining fabric
3. Ribbon for trim and binding

How to

1. Cut one body and one lining 7 inches by 7 inches.
2. Pin ribbons to right side of fabric as shown in sketch to form a pleasing pattern.
3. Stitch upper edge of ribbons. (Test tension of sewing machine to be sure ribbons do not pucker.)
4. Pin body of case and lining with right sides together.
5. Sew top edge only.
6. Turn and press.
7. Fold case in half, right side outside.
8. Stitch a ¼-inch seam on side and bottom edges.
9. Fold ribbon binding over raw edges, mitering corner, and top-stitch to finish.

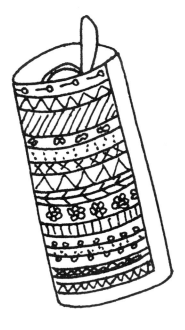

70

10. chicken potholder nesting on a scouring pad egg

A whimsical addition to any kitchen—and useful too!

Materials

1. Scraps of small-print quilted fabric, matching solid for underside lining and cotton batting for padding
2. ¾ yard bias tape
3. Scrap of jumbo rickrack
4. Two buttons
5. One yellow scouring pad
6. Cotton for stuffing

How to

1. Enlarge diagram and cut out two of pattern D in the print fabric.
2. Cut one solid lining and one cotton batting from pattern E.
3. Cut a 3-inch length of rickrack for comb of chicken.
4. Fold, pleat and pin comb to one head.
5. With right sides together and using a ¼-inch seam allowance, seam top pieces from A, across back to tail. Turn and trim seams. Using cotton, stuff head and neck.
6. Now pin cotton batting and lining to underside of open wings.
7. Bind raw edges with bias tape, making a loop on end of tail for hanging.
8. Sew on button eyes.
9. Set chicken on yellow scouring pad.

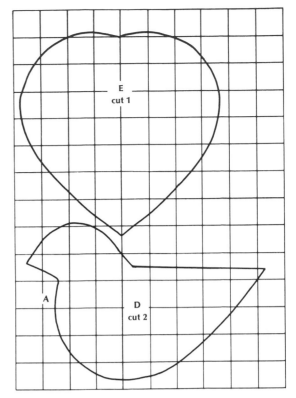

box = 1 sq. in.

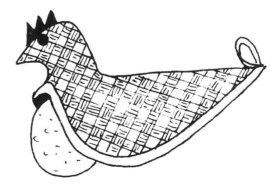

11. mother/daughter skirts

Gather up a batch of pretty prints or checks and sew a group of matching mother/ daughter hostess skirts!

FOR MOTHER

Materials

1. 5 yards of 39-inch-wide cotton fabric
2. 3½ yards cotton eyelet 2 inches wide
3. 3½ yards ribbon to thread through eyelet
4. 1 yard inch-wide elastic

How to

1. Cut three panels of cotton fabric 32 inches long by 39 inches wide.
2. Sew seams, using a ½-inch seam allowance.
3. Press seams open.
4. Turn upper edge to wrong side ¼ inch. Stitch down.
5. Turn again, 1¼ inches in, to form casing for elastic. Stitch at upper edge and then 1¼ inches below.
6. Thread elastic through casing and gather for a 25-inch-to-26-inch waist.
7. Hem skirt and then add a 9-inch *bias* ruffle to bottom of skirt. Finish off with eyelet and ribbon as is pictured.

FOR DAUGHTER

Materials

1. 2½ yards of 39-inch-wide cotton fabric
2. 1½ yards inch-wide eyelet
3. 1½ yards ribbon to thread through eyelet
4. ½ yard inch-wide elastic

How to

1. Cut two panels of cotton fabric 26 inches by 22 inches.
2. Follow steps 2 through 5 as in mother's skirt.
3. Thread elastic through casing and gather for a 17-inch waist.
4. Hem skirt and then add a 5-inch *bias* ruffle to bottom of skirt.
5. Finish off with eyelet and ribbon as is pictured.

72

12. ribbon sewing kit

I have this friend named Jane Collins who is superbly talented and the most creative person I have ever known. Also, she is the chairman (chairwoman?) of the Make-Do Board. Who else (when her gas stove was not connected) would *cook* an eight-pound salmon in the dishwasher (two cycles did it) or machine-wash and spin-dry her spinach for salad? She also finds items like the following when you're telling her you're writing a sewing book.

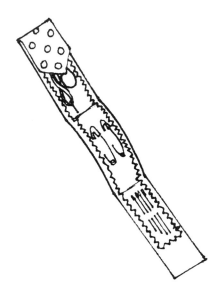

Materials

1. 17 inches of 1½-inch-wide grosgrain ribbon
2. 10 inches of 1-inch-wide cotton with pinked edge
3. Needles, pins, thread, snaps, safety pins, etc.
4. One small pearl button

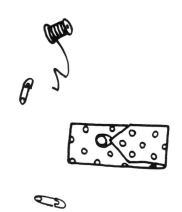

How to

1. Turn back edges of one end of ribbon and hand-stitch down. Make a small loop for the button at this end.
2. Glue a 2-inch by 1½-inch piece of cardboard to other end of ribbon, folding up end of ribbon so that cardboard does not show.
3. Place some pins, some needles with a small amount of varied colors of thread wound around them, some safety pins, etc., on the cotton strip and insert one end in cardboard end, hand-stitching it down.
4. Line up cotton strip with ribbon and fold over cardboard end until it is all wound up. Close by sewing on the button to fasten.

13. lapnaps

It's the thoughtful hostess who offers her guests extra-large lap napkins for buffet dinners. These are simple to make and are great impulse items. They normally sell at retail for about two dollars a napkin. If you can offer them for seventy-five cents to a dollar, these pretty napkins will cause the money to fall into your lap.

Materials

Almost any light- to medium-weight cotton fabric will do. So much the better if the fabric is Dacron and cotton or permanent press, for easy care. Gingham is great because it is easy to follow the checks for sewing.

How to

1.   Cut fabric into 26-inch squares. Finished lap nap is 24 inches square.
2.   Fold four edges to wrong side 1 inch and press.
3.   Sew corners, as illustrated, to miter.
4.   Clip and turn to right side.
5.   Turn raw edges under ¼ inch.
6.   Stitch with decorative patterned stitch such as open zigzag.

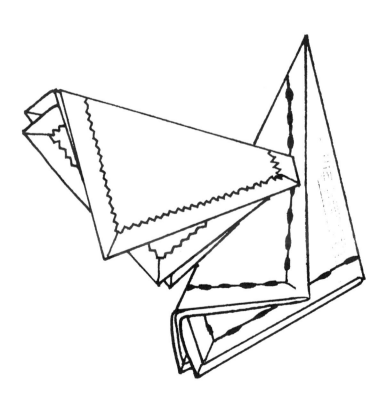

14. ribbon napkin rings

Here's a no-sewing project for nimble fingers that can cut and glue. Ribbon-trimmed napkin rings can be a pretty hostess gift or a charming summer party table accessory. I've used gingham ribbons and trimmed them with tiny embroidered French baby ribbon.

Materials

1. Ribbon, either gingham or striped. Generally a patterned ribbon is best. If you do use solid colors, try to get some with picot edges. Get 1½-inch-wide ribbon. One yard will make four napkin rings.
2. Some embroidered ribbon ½ inch wide
3. Tubing from empty toilet tissue or paper towel rolls
4. White glue such as Sobo or Elmer's, diluted with water

How to

1. Cut the tubing into 1½-inch pieces with a razor.
2. Measure the inside length of ribbon needed. Cut. Remeasure for the outside and cut ribbon to fit with ¼-inch overlap for a finished edge.
3. Dot on a very small amount of glue inside the ring. Ease in ribbon lining. Smooth with fingers.
4. Repeat for outside. Overlap edge of ribbon. Turn under and glue.
5. Glue the ½-inch embroidered ribbon around middle of napkin ring. Fill with pretty napkins to complement the rings and believe me, they will sell like hot cakes!

15. child's nightgown

A child-tested nightgown, warm and cozy, in pretty flannel or gingham. It will fit a toddler size 4.

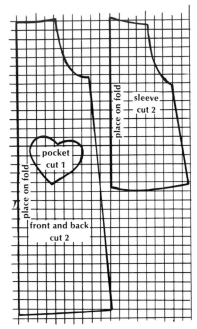

box = 1 sq. in.

Materials

1. 1 yard flowered or striped flannel, or gingham (for body of nightgown)
2. ½ yard same fabric in contrast color (for sleeves and pocket)
3. ⅔ yard of ½-inch bias tape
4. ½ yard of ¼-inch elastic

How to

1. Enlarge diagram and cut out pattern.
2. Make a ¼-inch hem in sleeve edges.
3. Sew bias tape to wrong side of sleeve 1¼ inches from sleeve edge to create a casing. Insert elastic. Repeat for other sleeve.
4. Pin sleeves to armhole edges of front and back with right sides together. Stitch.
5. Make a ¼-inch hem at neck edge. Sew bias tape to wrong side 1¼ inches from finished edge. Insert elastic.
6. Turn in pocket ¼ inch on all sides. Press. Pin pocket to front of gown as is shown and top-stitch in place.
7. Pin underarm and side seams and stitch from edge of hem to edge of sleeve.
8. Finish by putting in hem either by hand or with machine blind stitch. Make a bow for center of neckline, using a scrap of ¼-inch-wide ribbon.

76

16. tooth fairy pillowcase

A special pillowcase just for those exciting nights when the tooth fairy comes to exchange a baby tooth for silver coins.

Materials

1. Standard white or pastel pillowcase. (You might keep an eye out for special sales or irregulars.)
2. Small scraps of dress cottons, tiny florals, dots or mini gingham checks
3. Embroidery floss, and needles
4. Transfer paper and tracing or tissue paper

How to

1. Trace fairy design onto tissue paper.
2. With opening of pillowcase to the left, transfer the design, positioning fairy near pillow edge. Sew both fairy and tooth pocket according to picture design.
3. Using same tissue, cut out dress body of fairy from a small print fabric. Cut wings from another fabric.
4. Pin dress and wings in place. Stitch to pillow. Finish edges with zigzag stitch or hand embroidery.
5. Embroider face, hair, hands and magic wand.
6. Cut a 2-inch by 2-inch square to match fairy's dress. Turn in edges ¼ inch and press. Hem one side for the opening.
7. Position tooth pocket and stitch three sides to pillow.

Note: This might be a "pass-along" project. Have the cutting and machine sewing done by one person and then pass it along to your talented ladies who embroider well.

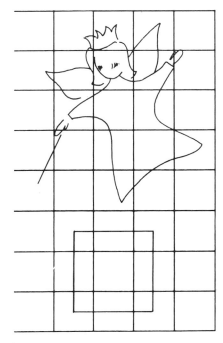

box = 1 sq. in.

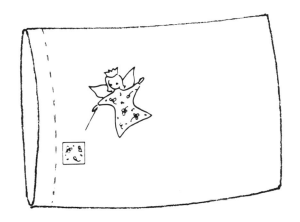

17. diet birthday cake bag

The young lady who stitched the samples for this book, Merle Altman, came in on my birthday with an idea so clever I thought it should be included here. For those of us on lifelong diets, it's a birthday cake that won't add an ounce! It's made of rickrack and canvas and has a zipper so that after the big day it's a perfect bag for hair curlers, cotton puffs or whatever needs a home.

Materials

1. ½ yard solid-color canvas
2. 24-inch-long zipper
3. 2 yards jumbo rickrack and 2 yards baby rickrack

How to

1. Cut two canvas circles 9 inches in diameter (top and bottom of cake) and a canvas piece 27 inches by 4½ inches (side of cake).
2. Pencil the words "Happy Birthday" on one of the canvas circles and embroider it, using the sewing machine. Trim by top-stitching both sizes of rickrack on the embroidered top and side of cake.
3. Starting 1½ inches from end, sew zipper on one side of long rectangular piece. Sew other side of zipper to plain circle.
4. Sew a back seam on rectangular piece and finish seaming bottom.
5. Unzip and sew non-zipper edge of rectangular piece to embroidered circle.
6. Having completed the Birthday Cake Bag, pink all edges inside to finish it off.

18. patched potholder and recipe-book cover

Gather up all your colorful cotton scraps to make this charming kitchen ensemble or buy patchwork by the yard to achieve the same effect.

POTHOLDER

Materials

1. Nine 2½-inch squares of printed cotton fabric
2. 7¼-inch square of backing fabric such as chintz
3. Two 7¼-inch felt squares
4. 1 yard double-fold bias tape

How to

1. Arrange and stitch the nine squares together to form a 7¼-inch square, using a ¼-inch seam allowance. Press seams flat.
2. Baste the felt squares to wrong side of backing material.
3. Place patched square on top of this with wrong side facing the felt side. Baste.
4. Stitch double-fold bias tape around all edges, forming a loop in one corner, and stitch in place.

RECIPE-BOOK COVER

Materials

1. Scraps of fabric (depends on size of recipe book to be covered)
2. Cotton fabric for book-cover lining
3. Inexpensive blank-paged recipe book

How to

1. Cut squares that measure 2 inches. Cut and sew together as many as are needed to cover recipe book, using a ¼-inch seam allowance.
2. Cut a lining that is 12 inches wider than the patched book cover.
3. Fold each end of the lining 3 inches in to what would be the center of the book. Then fold over again 3 inches, forming a finished pocket flap. Pin and baste.
4. With right sides together, stitch patched cover and lining together, leaving a 4-inch opening for turning. Turn; stitch closed.
5. Slip cover onto book.

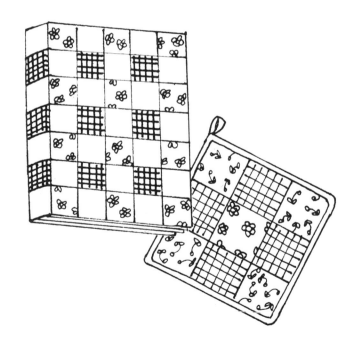

19. telephone book and message clipboard

How many times do you look around for something on which to write a telephone message and there's not a piece of paper in sight? Add a giant yellow pad to this clipboard and you'll never have that problem again.

TELEPHONE BOOK

Materials

1. Inexpensive personal telephone book
2. Enough fabric and lining to cover book

How to

1. Cut cover to fit entire outside of book, adding ½ inch for book seam allowance.
2. Follow steps 2 through 5 in the instructions given for the Recipe-Book Cover.

MESSAGE CLIPBOARD

Materials

1. Inexpensive clipboard from the dime store
2. Enough fabric to entirely cover clipboard

How to

1. Unscrew clip from board. Make a pillowcase for the board, cutting one open end longer to go over top of board to the back.

Glue this end down and finish off with a bit of trim.
2. Screw clip back on board.

80

20. needlepoint tote

With all the "needlepoint nuts" around these days, you will be sure to sell out of this item quickly. It's a handy carryall for needlepoint necessities. Also, the use of ribbon inside to hold different-color yarns makes it an easy-to-sew project.

Materials

1. Tote: 30-inch by 17-inch piece of plaid seersucker
   30-inch by 17-inch piece of solid-color canvas (for lining)
   30-inch by 17-inch piece of cotton batting
2. Pockets: 14-inch by 8½-inch piece of solid-color canvas
   5-inch by 4-inch piece of solid-color canvas
   4-inch by 3-inch piece of solid-color canvas
3. Handles: two strips 20 inches by 2 inches in plaid seersucker
4. Two 22-inch-long zippers (color to match lining)
5. 1½ yards double-fold bias tape (color to match lining)
6. ⅔ yard of 1-inch grosgrain ribbon

How to

1. Turn top of pocket edges under ½ inch and hem with a zigzag stitch. Turn rest of pocket edges under ½ inch and top-stitch in place to lining according to sketch, remembering to leave top edge open. (Stuff smallest pocket with cotton to act as a "needle cushion" and fill the next in size with a pair of embroidery scissors.)

2. Cut ribbon in half and top-stitch to lining, making 2-inch ribbon "loops" for holding yarn.
3. Sew plaid seersucker and layer of cotton batting together.
4. Fold the two handle strips in half lengthwise and top-stitch down on either side. Top-stitch each handle on either side of tote (outside).
5. Sew lining and outside part of tote together, top-stitching around all outside edges.
6. Fold tote in half and sew one zipper, starting at the bottom open edge of one side. Sew other zipper on other side. When zipped closed, the two zippers should meet at the center top of the tote near the handles.
7. Finish off outside raw zipper edges with double-fold bias tape.

21. sewing apron

I think this is a dandy idea. It's guaranteed to keep track of all loose sewing aids and what home sewer doesn't need that? (It's been measured for a 25-inch waistline.)

Materials

¾ yard solid-color canvas

How to

1. Enlarge diagram and cut out pattern, remembering to place side of apron on the *fold* of the fabric.

2. Hem all edges of apron with a ¼-inch top-stitched hem.

3. Turn under all pockets and scissors-holder tabs ¼ inch and then ¼ inch again and top-stitch on according to sketch.

4. Cut a 3¼-inch-wide strip 45 inches long. Fold in half for a waistband. Baste and top-stitch waistband on apron, leaving equal ends at sides for ties.

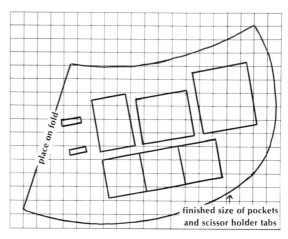

box = 1 sq. in.

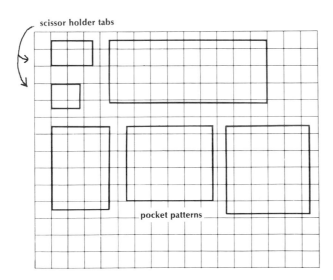

22. ribbon pillows

Stitch up a batch of these pretty gingham pillows, using coordinating ribbons in checks, stripes or dots.

Materials for one

1. Two 12-inch by 18-inch pieces of gingham *or* two 12-inch squares of gingham. (You might want to make the two sides of the pillows look different by using either different-size or different-color checks.)

2. Two pieces of 1-inch-to-2-inch wide ribbon cut into 12-inch lengths. (Here again, you may want to reverse colors or patterns.)

3. Pillow stuffing.

How to

1. Pin a strip of ribbon along each pillow section, approximately 3 inches from edge.

2. Stitch along edges of ribbon, using a zigzag stitch. Press.

3. Put two pillow sections together with right sides facing, and pin.

4. Stitch on all four sides with a ½-inch seam allowance but leave a 4-inch opening on one edge. Turn.

5. Stuff pillow and slip-stitch opening closed.

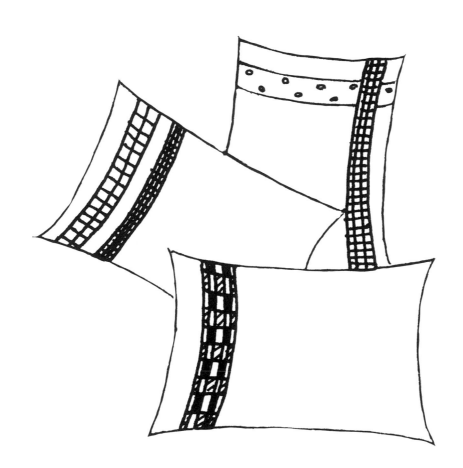

men's booth

One of the handsomest color combinations I know of is navy, brown and white (or beige) and that's why I've chosen it for the men's booth. The items are geared agewise from a teen-ager to a man in retirement . . . and that's pleasing a lot of people. Here's hoping you like each and every one of them.

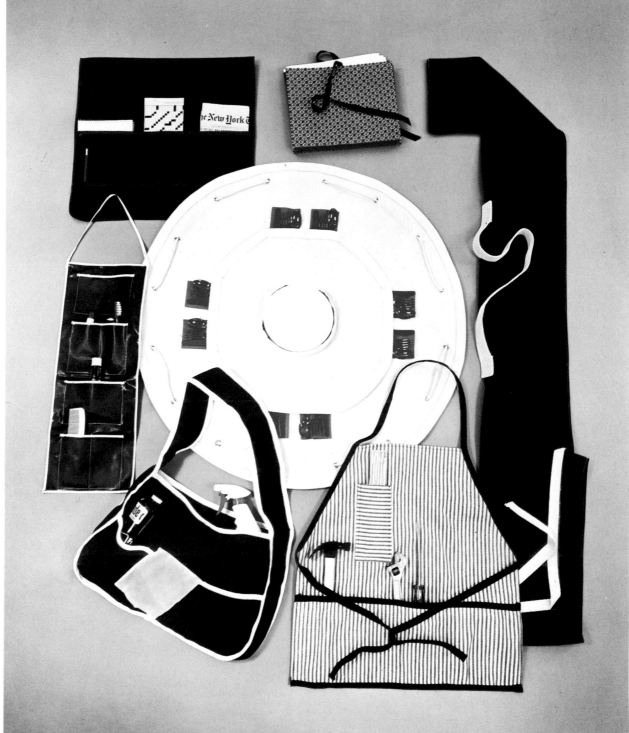

25. father-to-be bag

Here's a charming gift for the father-to-be from the mother-to-be. A lifesaver of a package with all types of items he will need while waiting at the hospital. It would hold such things as his favorite magazine, cigarettes, change for the telephone, a list of phone numbers, fruit, cookies, aspirin, tranquilizers and maybe even a few cigars!

Materials

1. ½ yard beige burlap or canvas
2. ½ yard red cotton lining
3. 6-inch square of red felt
4. Drawstring pouch for change
5. Note pad for numbers
6. Pillbox

How to

1. Cut out two pieces in burlap, 12 inches by 15 inches.
   Cut out one gusset in burlap, 6 inches by 42 inches.
   Cut out two pieces in red cotton, 12 inches by 15 inches.
   Cut out one gusset in red cotton, 6 inches by 42 inches.
   Cut out two burlap strips for handles, 4 inches by 14 inches.
   Cut out one 6-inch cross in red felt.
2. Using zigzag stitch, appliqué red cross to one piece of 12-inch by 15-inch burlap only.
3. Sew burlap gusset piece to both pieces of 12-inch by 15-inch burlap, using a ½-inch seam allowance. Trim corners, turn and press seams flat. Follow same procedure for red cotton lining pieces, using a 5/8-inch seam allowance.
4. Place lining inside bag and tack around top edge.
5. Fold down top edge of burlap bag ½ inch and then ½ inch again and top-stitch. You may top-stitch around edges of bag but this is optional.
6. Fold burlap handle strips in half lengthwise and sew raw edge, using a ½-inch seam allowance. Trim, turn and top-stitch edges. Attach to inside edges of bag as sketched.
7. Fill with a note pad, a drawstring pouch for change, and a pillbox with pills. The mother-to-be can add the rest!

26. accordion bill file

Here's a handsome way for dad to keep his bills and other important papers organized.

Materials

1. ⅛-inch-thick cardboard
2. Accordion file
3. ½ yard heavy printed cotton
4. 1½ yards 1-inch grosgrain ribbon
5. Elmer's Glue or Sobo

How to

1. Cut top flap from accordion file and discard. Sand the cut edge.
2. Cut cardboard to fit each flat side of accordion file.
3. Cut fabric the size of cardboard pieces plus 1½-inch allowance on all edges.

4. Apply glue to cardboard. When tacky, place cardboard on center of fabric and weigh down with some heavy books until dry. Miter corners and glue fabric allowance to underside of cardboard.
5. Cut ribbon in half and glue 5 inches of each strip to file covers.
6. Apply glue to file and attach the covered cardboard. Weigh and let dry.
7. Fill and tie ribbon in bow to hold file together.

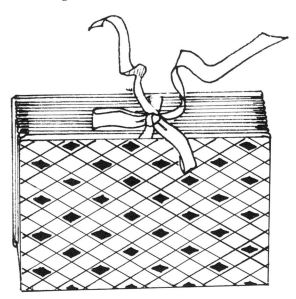

27. locker caddy

Every man who has a locker at work or wherever he enjoys sports would appreciate a place to put all the little extras such as keys, combs, cigarettes, etc., and that's why the locker caddy was made for him.

Materials

1. Caddy: 28-inch by 9½-inch piece of canvas
2. Pockets: Two 7-inch by 9-inch pieces of canvas
3. 2½ yards of ½-inch fold-over contrasting binding
4. Small inexpensive mirror

How to

1. Turn pockets under ½ inch on all sides and baste. Top-stitch binding on top of pockets only. Top-stitch pockets on caddy as is pictured.
2. Bind off all edges with binding.
3. Glue on mirror.
4. Punch a hole through top of caddy and insert wire clothes hanger to hang.

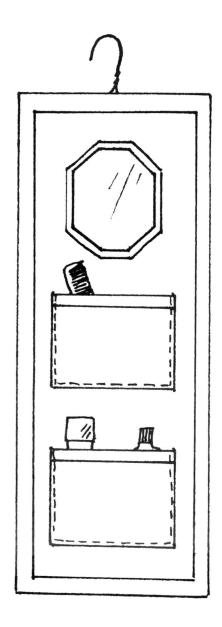

28. bedside caddy

We all know people who have been laid up with a broken bone or a bad back. The bedside caddy is for them. It is made to fit over the back of a chair but it could be placed between the box springs and mattress to hang down on one side of the bed. It houses a paperback of the moment, crossword puzzle, Kleenex and whatever else might help pass the time more pleasantly.

Materials

1. Sturdy canvas: 30 inches by 20 inches for caddy
20 inches by 4 inches for one pocket
20 inches by 10 inches for second pocket
2. 2½ yards matching double-fold bias tape
3. 1 yard of ½-inch contrasting fold-over bias tape

How to

1. Fold back the 30-inch by 20-inch piece of canvas so that it is 20 inches by 20 inches, to form cover for chair back. Top-stitch edges together.
2. Use contrasting bias trim and finish off one side of the long edge of both pockets.
3. Put large pocket on front of caddy and then smaller pocket on top of that, as is pictured. Top-stitch all three pieces together around the edge of caddy.
4. Bind all edges around with matching bias tape.
5. Top-stitch pockets vertically.

29. carpenter's apron

Men's aprons are meant to be useful. Here's a carpenter's apron with lots of small pockets for nuts, bolts, hammers, screwdrivers, etc.

Materials

1. 1 yard canvas or striped denim
2. 4 yards sturdy 1-inch fold-over tape

How to

1. Enlarge diagram and cut out pattern.
2. Cut a long, narrow pocket 8 inches by 4 inches. Turn in on all sides and baste. Sew this narrow pocket vertically on top part of apron, leaving top edge open to insert a carpenter's ruler.
3. Cut out a pocket 27 inches by 9 inches. Sew a piece of 1-inch fold-over tape along the top edge (lengthwise) of the pocket. Baste this pocket to the apron, matching side and bottom edges. Sew two vertical lines of stitching in pocket to form three sections. Finish off bottom edge with fold-over tape.
4. Turn outside edges of apron along top, arm and side edges in ¼ inch, then ½ inch, and top-stitch.
5. Stitch tape to neckline and arm edges to form halter. Sew rest of tape on sides for ties as is pictured.

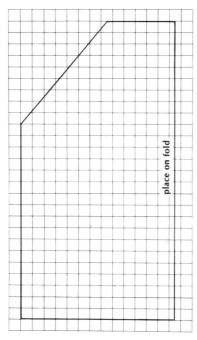

place on fold

box = 1 sq. in.

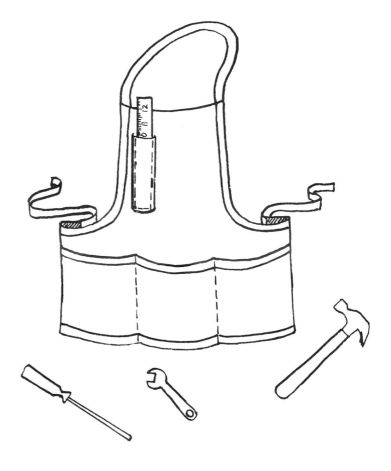

94

30. shoe cleaning caddy/car cleaning caddy

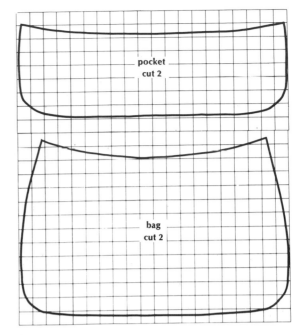

box = 1 sq. in.

Step-saving caddies to sling over his shoulder will keep all his supplies right at hand when he needs them.

Materials

1. ⅞ yard canvas
2. 3 yards double-fold bias binding in contrasting (or twill tape)
3. Stencils—paint or dye

How to

1. Enlarge diagram and cut out pattern pieces: cut two bags, two pockets, and gusset approximately 93 inches by 3 inches (may be pieced).
2. Stitch binding across top edge of both pockets. Then stitch one pocket onto each side of caddy as is shown, with two vertical lines of stitching to make separate compartments.
3. Stitch gusset pieces together at ends.
4. Stitch gusset onto one side of caddy, then onto other side, with wrong sides together, using ¼-inch seams.
5. Bind off each side of caddy and gusset/strap with bias binding or twill tape.
6. Stencil words on caddy such as "Shoe Caddy" or "Car Caddy." One title to a bag, however.

Note: The bag measures approximately 20 inches by 12 inches with a 3-inch-by-93-inch-long gusset/strap to hang diagonally across the body so it won't slip off while work is being done.

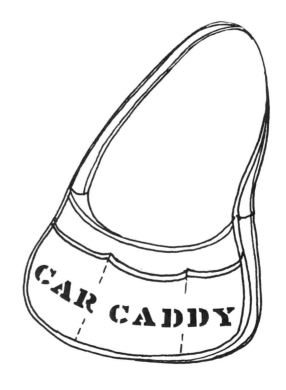

95

31. bridge table checkerboard

This is a giant-size version of checkers that will delight anybody. "Board" fits the top of any standard bridge table.

Materials for one set

1. 1 yard navy felt or oilcloth; ¼ yard white felt or oilcloth
2. Twenty-four jar lids (from 7-ounce Planter's peanut jars or equivalent)
3. Navy and white spray paint
4. 1 yard of ½-inch elastic
5. Plastic bag

How to

1. Cut one piece of navy felt the size of a bridge table, 30 inches by 30 inches.
2. Cut white felt into thirty-two 3-inch squares.
3. Copying checkerboard, glue white squares onto navy felt, leaving navy spaces to form a checkerboard. Do this in center of mat, leaving a 3-inch border all the way around.
4. Using a tight zigzag (appliqué) machine stitch and white thread, sew glued squares down, using the zigzag to also finish off edges of navy squares.
5. Attach a 5-inch piece of elastic diagonally on each corner of cloth to hold cloth onto bridge table.
6. Spray-paint twelve jar lids navy, twelve white, and package set in a plastic bag.

32. lap hugger

We all know what it's like to get settled under a lap robe only to discover that the TV guide, your eyeglasses or favorite paperback book are nowhere within reaching distance. This unique lap robe with pockets (it *deserves* to be called a lap hugger) solves that problem once and for all!

Materials

1. 1 yard heavyweight camel-color woolen fabric, 45 inches wide
2. 9 yards heavy brown binding, ½-inch-wide fold-over
3. Navy felt pockets: 11½ inches by 7½ inches; 7 inches by 6½ inches. Brown felt pockets: 10 inches by 8 inches; 8½ inches by 5 inches.

How to

1. Lay out wool fabric and pin on four strips of brown binding the *length* of the lap hugger. Open flat the fold-over binding to do so and top-stitch down according to sketch. (Note that the two outer strips go only 33 inches of the length, however.)
2. Using the same binding, bind off all edges of the lap hugger by folding it over and top-stitching.
3. Turn under all edges of pockets ½ inch. Top-stitch the *top edge only* of each pocket. Then pin on pockets according to sketch. Top-stitch in place, remembering to leave top edge of pockets open.

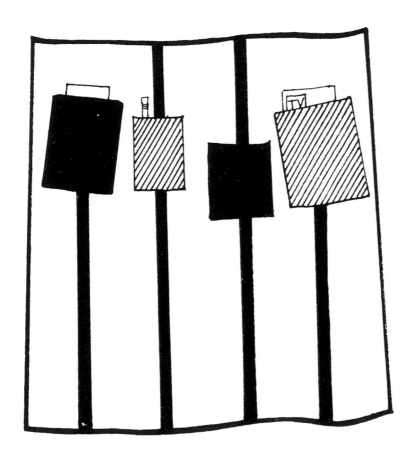

33. shower tote

This is a great gift for the men's booth. It can be for anyone, depending on fabric and color choice. Choose from vinyl-coated cotton, canvas or duck. A long, narrow tote with multiple pockets for soap, shampoo and grooming aids.

Materials

1. Sturdy fabric approximately 48 inches by 8 inches
2. Heavy bias-fold tape in contrasting color

How to

1. Cut a long, narrow strip of fabric 25 inches by 8 inches.
2. Cut four pockets: two 4½ inches by 6½ inches; two 5½ inches by 6½ inches.
3. Bind top edge of each pocket with bias tape. Fold tape over edge and stitch.
4. Fold under other three edges of pockets, press and pin to long piece of fabric as shown.
5. Stitch pockets in place.
6. Trim all edges of shower tote with bias tape. Stitch in place.
7. Cut a piece of tape 18 inches long. Pin and stitch to back of tote at top to hang on shower head.

Note: If you choose to make this shower tote, you might offer to stencil two or three initials to upper edge as shown. This could be done while the customer waits if materials are on hand.

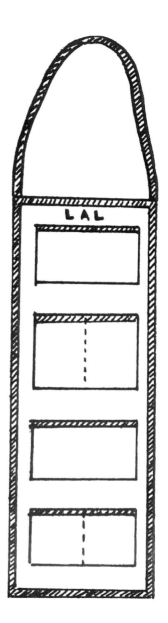

34. silverware camping caddy

Anyone who camps knows how handy this item can be. There's no need ever for lost silverware with a silverware camping caddy. You could also make a larger version for cooking implements such as soup ladles, tongs, long forks and pancake turners.

Materials

1. 18½ inch by 15 inch navy canvas lining

2. 18½ inch by 7 inch navy canvas pocket

3. 18½ inch by 15 inch navy/white cotton check

4. 18½ inch by 15 inch cotton batting

5. 1 yard of ½ inch navy grosgrain ribbon

6. 2 yards navy fold-over bias tape

How to

1. Take the navy canvas pocket and make a 1-inch hem the length of one side of it. Put this pocket on top of the navy canvas lining so that the raw edges of the two meet at the long bottom side. Baste together.

2. Top-stitch vertical lines 1 inch apart down the entire length of the pocket. (This is to hold the silverware.)

3. Take the navy check and the cotton batting and baste together.

4. Lay the pocket/lining piece face up on the cotton batting/navy-check piece. The cotton batting is in the center. Baste around all edges. Stitch. Finish off edges with navy fold-over bias tape.

6. Fold top third of silverware caddy down to the inside.

7. With the top folded down, attach center of navy ribbon to center of navy check for ties to close silverware caddy once it is filled and rolled up.

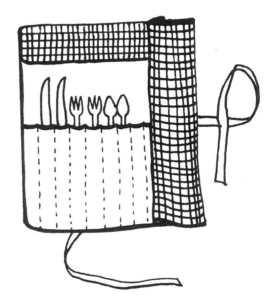

37. drawstring bag for laundry or books

Here's another simple moneymaker. The old drawstring laundry bag, but new-looking if the fabric is part of the overall color theme of the booth. Or, made up in a sturdy bright-color canvas (then it fits into the bright, solid-color children's booth), it can be stenciled at the bazaar with the buyer's initials and used for books or gym equipment as well as laundry!

Materials

1. Canvas that measures 27 inches by 56 inches
2. 5 feet of rope
3. Dye to contrast with fabric
4. Stencils for bold initials

How to

1. Fold fabric in half, right sides together, and sew sides. Press seams open.
2. Turn to right side and press.
3. Fold top edge ½ inch under and then fold again 2½ inches. Pin. Stitch, forming a casing.
4. At one side seam, make a 2-inch slit in casing exterior and insert rope. After threading rope through, knot both ends to form loop for hanging bag on a hook.

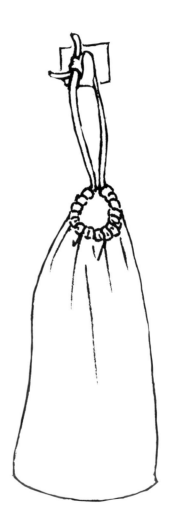

38. traveling shoe bag

A simple sewing project and one that is easily suitable for ladies or men, depending on the fabric selection. Gingham or calico for the ladies; felt or canvas for the gentlemen.

Materials

1. Shoe bag yardage: 12 inches by 24 inches (ladies); 16 inches by 30 inches (men)
2. 1-inch bias tape for casings
3. 1¼ yards ribbon or cord for drawstring
4. 8-inch by 10-inch felt piece

How to

1. Cut a 16-inch by 30-inch (men) or 12-inch by 24-inch (women) piece of fabric.
2. Cut two felt footprints. (Use a pair of inner soles for a pattern.)
3. Place the two felt footprints at one end of fabric, leaving ample room for the casing and drawstring. Top-stitch or zigzag stitch in place as is pictured.
4. Then fold fabric in half, right sides together.
5. Stitch sides, leaving a ½-inch seam allowance.
6. Trim corners. Press seams open.
7. Turn edges at top inside ¼ inch. Baste. Fold down again ¼ inch and stitch down.
8. Pin casing 2 inches down from top edge. Stitch both edges. Turn bag right side out.
9. Stitch down center below casing to lower edge, forming two pockets.

10. Thread cord or ribbon through casing, tying in a bow to close.

39. towel wrap skirt

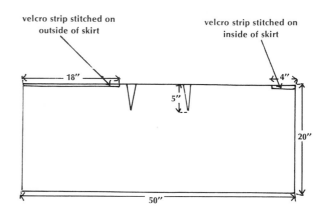

I know a little eight-year-old girl who made this towel wrap skirt for her father for Father's Day (great for getting out of the shower) in a bright turquoise blue terry cloth. He has worn it so much he told me that he has worn it out!

Materials

1. One bath towel
2. ½ yard Velcro

How to

1. Cut out towel according to measurements of diagram. (The use of Velcro makes this a "one size fits all" garment.)
2. Make two darts (1 inch deep) that taper to 5 inches in length. Make each dart 20 inches from its respective end.
3. Make a 1-inch machine hem on all four sides.
4. Sew a 14-inch strip of Velcro to *outside* top edge of skirt, according to diagram. Sew a 4-inch piece of Velcro to inside top edge, following diagram.
5. A large patch pocket can be added to front of skirt or embroidered initials if so desired.

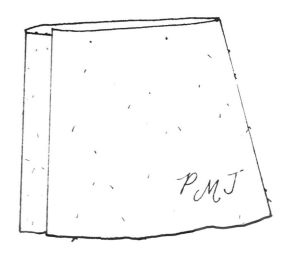

40. ski bag

For anybody and everybody who skis these days, this could be a best seller. It's a bag to house skis and is so simple to make you'll be mad at yourself for not having thought of it first!

Materials

1.   One piece of heavy canvas 90 inches long and 20 inches wide (2½ yards)
2.   2 yards *very heavy* woven tape

How to

1.   Fold canvas lengthwise and stitch one end closed as well as along one entire side, using a ⅝-inch seam allowance. Turn; press.
2.   Hem open edge, making a 1½-inch hem.
3.   Top-stitch in a contrast-color thread on the outside along side, and bottom of ski bag for decorative purposes.
4.   Attach the *ends* of 1 yard of tape in middle of bag to act as handle. Attach the center only of the other yard of tape to top edge (about 6 inches down from open end) of bag. This is to act as a pair of ties with which to close ski bag once skis have been put inside.

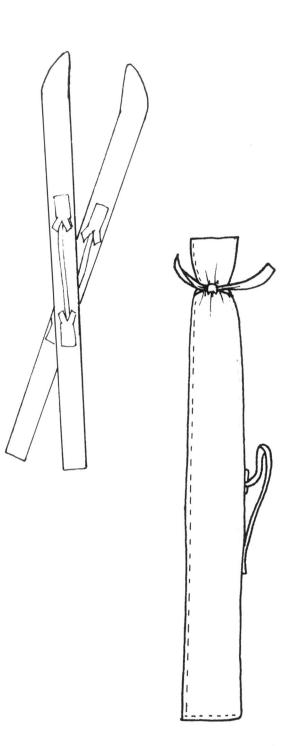

41. picture frames on ribbon

Here's a fast-sell item. Three small picture frames (dime-store variety) hanging on a ribbon from a brass ring. All that's needed are the family pictures.

Materials

1. 1 yard of 1-inch-wide grosgrain ribbon
2. One brass ring (1½-inch-diameter)
3. Three round lightweight wood picture frames (4-inch-diameter). They can also be square or rectangular frames. Just keep the size small.

How to

1. Cut a 25-inch-long piece of ribbon to hold frames.
2. Sew one end of ribbon over ring and with scissors fish-tail other end.
3. Hang frames, using glue-on picture hangers, on ribbon, spacing them 2½ inches apart as is pictured.

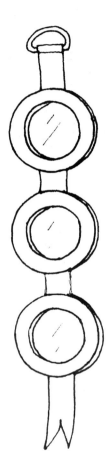

42. tennis racket cover

Tennis, anyone? This is a snappy, new-looking cover idea for the tennis fans who seem to be sprouting up everywhere these days.

Materials

1. ½ yard canvas
2. 20-inch neckline zipper
3. Bias-covered cording and ½-inch bias binding to match
4. Two large snaps
5. One small terry-cloth towel
6. ½ yard of 1-inch-wide webbing

How to

1. Enlarge diagram and cut out pattern, cutting two pieces for the racket.
2. Cut gusset strip 1½ inches by 18 inches. Cut another strip 7½ inches by 7½ inches to be pocket for tennis balls and towel.
3. Cut racket cover neck facing, 1½ inches by 8 inches.
4. Stitch bottom end of zipper to one end of gusset.
5. Attach cording around front piece and back piece of racket cover.
6. Stitch one side of gusset and zipper to one side of racket cover, using a ¼-inch seam allowance. Repeat for other side of cover.
7. Attach cording to neck facing opening.
8. With right sides together, stitch neck facing to opening of cover. Turn to inside, tacking ends to zipper.
9. Finish off ends of pocket piece with bias binding, as is shown in sketch.

10. Turn under pocket sides ½ inch. Top-stitch pocket sides to racket cover.
11. Cut a 15-inch length of webbing and fold end under, top-stitching end of strip to pocket near neck of racket cover. Measure 3 inches down and sew a snap attaching it to pocket. This is to hold the small terry-cloth towel.
12. Fold under other end of strip and fasten with a snap to hold tennis balls in place.
13. Sew a small loop of bias binding at top center for tennis racket to hang on a hook when not in use.

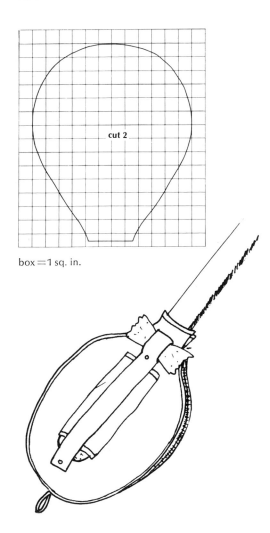

cut 2

box = 1 sq. in.

43. man's necktie

The biggest-selling pattern of all time in the home-sewing market has been the man's necktie and that's the reason for it here. Our thinking is that it makes sense to tie into a good thing!

Materials

1. Tie fabric: silk, linen, cotton, lightweight wool, acetate, blend or just about any fabric imaginable—⅝ yard of 45-inch fabric makes one tie 3½ inches wide

2. Interfacing: ½ yard Tie-Shape

3. Lining: ¼ yard China silk or SiBonne

How to

All tie pieces must be cut on true bias.

1. Cut one each of pattern piece A and B in tie fabric. Cut one each of pattern piece C and D in tie interfacing. Cut one each of pattern piece E and F in tie lining.

2. Press under ⅜-inch seam allowance on tie front and tie-front lining. Slash as indicated on pattern and be careful to miter corners. (See Diagram 1.)

3. Pin lining on fabric, wrong sides together. Slip-stitch in place. Press. (Diagram 2.)

4. Do same for tie back and tie-back lining.

5. With right sides together, stitch tie front to tie back (⅜-inch seam allowance) at center back seam. Press open.

6. Working on a flat surface, place interfacing in center of tie. Baste interfacing to center back seam allowance. (Diagram 3.)

7. Fold tie over interfacing. Press lightly —do not press flat. Slip-stitch in place, catching tie interfacing. Do not pull thread tightly, since bias stretches and the thread might break. (Diagram 4.) And that's all there is to it!

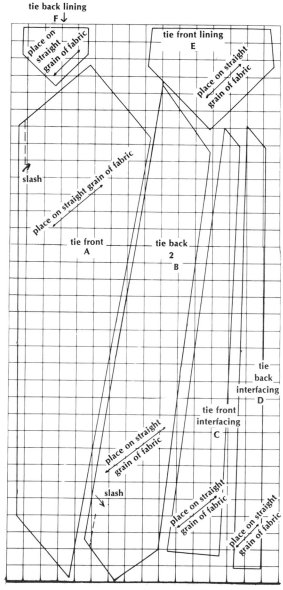

box = 1 sq. in.

1

2

3

4

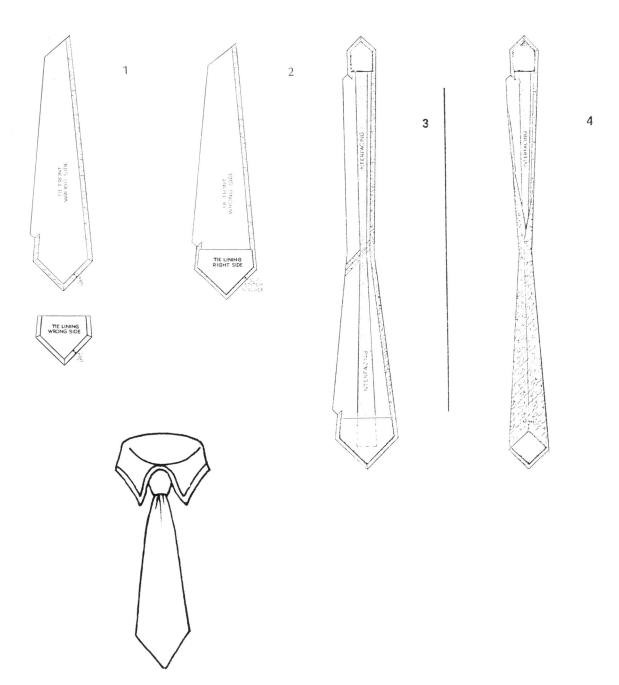

TIE FRONT
WRONG SIDE

TIE FRONT
WRONG SIDE

TIE LINING
RIGHT SIDE

TIE LINING
WRONG SIDE

INTERFACING

INTERFACING

INTERFACING

44. beach towel with pockets

Everybody knows that going to the beach means lugging a lot of extras besides a bathing suit and towel. So we designed a beach towel with pockets to solve the problem. Suntan lotion, sunglasses and your favorite paperback will always be in reach.

Materials

1. One large beach towel
2. One matching or contrast-color bath towel
3. 2 yards Velcro

How to

1. Cut off both ends of bath towel to fit across one end of beach towel.
2. Fold bath towel in half lengthwise and sew up both ends. Turn right side out and top-stitch.
3. Top-stitch one long edge of bath towel to one end of beach towel. Sew a strip of Velcro on top of this top-stitching.
4. Sew the other strip of Velcro to the other edge of the bath towel.
5. Divide bath towel into three separate pockets with two vertical lines of top-stitching.

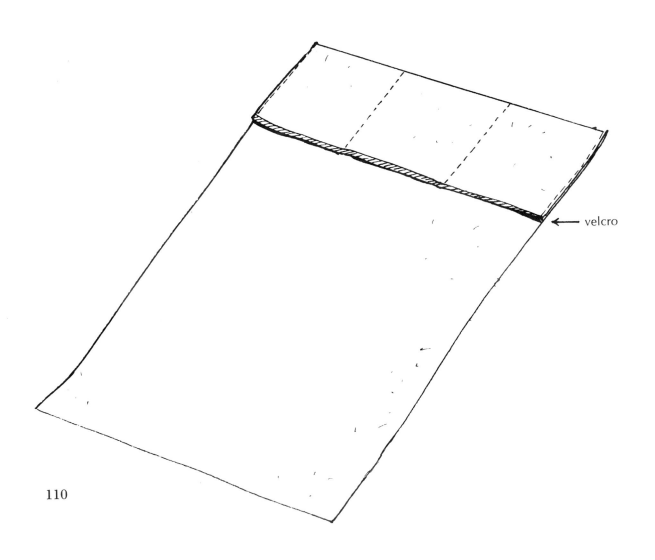

velcro

45. personalized brick doorstop

Are you ready for another *easy* idea? How about brand-new bricks that you just stencil with the customers' initials right at the booth? You need nothing more than a wheelbarrow full of bricks, a stencil and a small can of black shiny paint. I bet you sell out of them before you can spell "brick doorstop" backward!

46. modern fabric painting

This is one of the greatest ideas of all time. Simply buy 1 yard of a giant modern cotton print (the Scandinavian countries outdo themselves when it comes to this kind of fabric) and frame it in a modern chrome frame. Believe me, it's a very simple but a most effective way to decorate. And it has to be the easiest idea in this book!

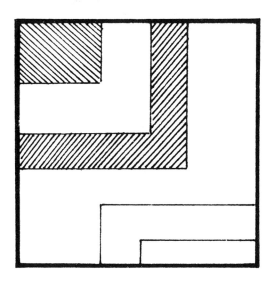

children's booth

The ideas for what to put in a children's booth came fast and furious, and so did the colors. What could be more natural than the crayon colors of bright red, yellow, green and blue? Also, a lot of our designs came from coloring books, which is a suggestion I'd like to pass on to you. Now go ahead and have fun. You'll be amazed at what you can do.

49. giraffe growing chart

A child can enjoy watching his growth as it is marked on this clever chart. It's a one-of-a-kind and may well be the first to sell out so maybe you had better think of this idea by the dozen.

Materials

1. Red vinyl strip 12 inches by 36 inches
2. Yellow vinyl length 8 inches by 24 inches for giraffe
3. Small vinyl pieces—green, yellow, brown
4. One wide tape measure
5. Sobo or Elmer's Glue
6. Two 12-inch rulers
7. 3½ yards green double-fold bias tape
8. Press-on Pellon 12 inches by 36 inches

How to

1. Enlarge diagram and cut out giraffe, leaves and sun patterns.
2. Scotch-tape the pattern to the vinyl, and cut out a yellow giraffe, brown spots, green leaves, yellow sun. (Don't use pins, for the pinholes will show.)
3. Glue spots to giraffe. Then glue mouth and eyelashes.
4. Press Pellon to back of red vinyl strip. Bind two sides of red vinyl strip with green binding.
5. Make a casing at the top of red vinyl strip. Fold vinyl back 1½ inches and stitch down. Insert a 12-inch ruler. Repeat for bottom of vinyl strip.
6. Glue giraffe to vinyl strip. Glue on leaves and sun.
7. Glue on tape measure beginning at 20 inches at bottom.
8. Stitch a piece of bias tape to ends of top strip to form a cord for hanging.
9. Include a card with Growing Chart, suggesting that the chart be measured accurately from floor when it is hung up.

box = 1 sq. in.

118

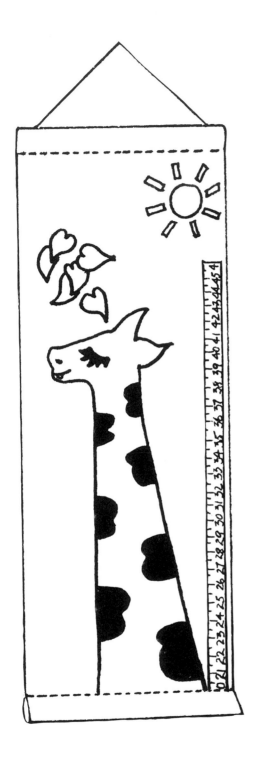

50. rainy day grab bag

Jazzy-looking paper bags filled with things to keep the kids busy and save the day for mother!

Materials

1. Small-size paper bags
2. Red rickrack or trim for girls; blue rickrack or trim for boys
3. Glue
4. Assorted dime-store toys: Yo-Yo, jacks, marbles, puzzles, car, plane, doll, animals, etc. (or candies)
5. Marking pen

How to

1. Write ''grab bag'' on each bag.
2. Glue appropriate rickrack along top of bag.
3. Fill with little toys and things to eat, all designed to keep the children busy and happy.

119

51. hippo and el toro place mats

You'll never wonder where your napkin is with these bright and colorful place mats that are made from oilcloth cutouts with a brass curtain ring as a napkin holder!

Materials for four

1. ⅝ yard of 46-inch-wide oilcloth or vinyl
2. ⅜ yard each of two contrasting colors of oilcloth for appliqué
3. Four 2-inch-diameter brass curtain rings
4. Sobo or Elmer's glue
5. 7 yards double-fold bias tape

How to

1. Cut four mats 12 inches by 18 inches from ⅝ yard piece. (If oilcloth or vinyl is too lightweight, cut four pieces of interfacing and four pieces of Stitch Witchery to same measurements.) Press to wrong side of vinyl.
2. Finish off edges with bias tape.
3. Enlarge diagrams for appliqué patterns. Cut two toros and two hippos from contrasting colors.
4. Glue pieces to mats.
5. Sew a brass ring to each nose to hold napkin.

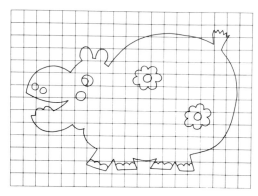

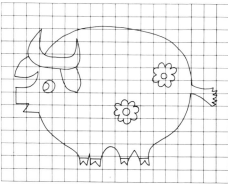

box = 1 sq. in.

120

52. tub tote

Handy tub tote will hold child's toys as well as shampoo, combs and brushes. It's easy to make and will be just as easy to sell.

Materials

1.   Metal towel bar 12 inches to 24 inches long, with suction cup on each end
2.   Terry-cloth towel the width of towel bar

How to

1.   The width of the tote depends on the length of the bar you use. Cut a piece of terry cloth as wide as the bar plus ½ inch on each side for hemming. Make this piece 8 inches long.
2.   Cut a second piece of terry cloth 1 inch less in width and 2 inches shorter in length, using selvage of towel along top edge.
3.   Make a ½-inch hem on the sides and bottom of both pieces.
4.   Top-stitch the two pieces together down the two sides and across the bottom, keeping right sides facing up.
5.   Sew vertical seams through both pieces to form three pockets about the same size.
6.   To attach the tote to the towel bar, sew the flap of fabric at the top of the tote over the bar.

53. styrofoam crayon caddy

Colorful crayon caddy keeps crayons well organized and prevents their breaking. It's a great idea for the nonsewer who wants to help out.

Materials

1.   Styrofoam block approximately 3 inches high by 10 inches wide by 4 inches deep
2.   Box of crayons
3.   Red, yellow, blue or green spray paint
4.   Stencil (optional)

How to

1.   Punch holes with letter opener or any sharp object the width of a crayon. Evenly align the holes in the block. Make the number of holes depend upon the number of crayons you are using.
2.   Spray-paint entire block. Allow to dry thoroughly.
3.   Insert crayons with pointed ends up.
4.   Stencil child's name on sides of the crayon caddy at the booth.

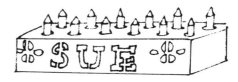

121

54.   baby's birth-date blanket

A charming baby blanket appliquéd with a train for the boys and a flower bed for the girls. All that's needed is for the customer to take felt-tip pen in hand and print in the newborn's vital statistics!

Materials

1.   Inexpensive lightweight baby blanket
2.   Washable multicolored scraps of fabric

How to

1.   Enlarge diagram and cut out train or floral design in multicolored scraps of fabric.
2.   Baste design to blanket and appliqué on, using the zigzag stitch on the sewing machine.
3.   Sell blanket with embroidery floss or with a felt-tip pen for customer to fill in the name, date and weight of the baby.

design for girls

design for boys

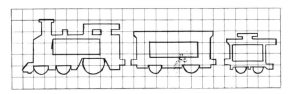

box = 1 sq. in.

122

55. child's vest

Here is an easy project for your volunteers. No sewing—just careful cutting. Simply cut out a vest and colorful felt designs for trim. Younger children can glue the designs where they like, while older ones can sew or embroider them on. I suggest you package this in a plastic bag and include a card explaining how to put the vest together. It might be a good idea to make one up so people can see what they get when they buy the plastic bag packet. This fits a size 8.

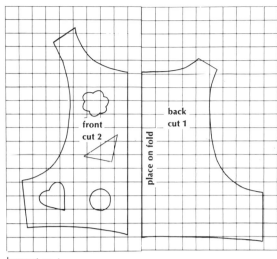

box = 1 sq. in.

Materials

1. ½ yard felt for vest
2. Felt and trim remnants in bright colors

How to

1. Enlarge diagram and cut out pattern. Pattern given here is for a child's size 8.
2. Place back of pattern on fold of fabric. Front pattern piece is cut double.
3. Pin and cut out.
4. Cut out designs of contrasting colors.
5. Write out card with instructions:

Make Your Own Vest!
1. Pin front sections to back at shoulder and underarm. Stitch together, using a ½-inch seam allowance.
2. Turn to inside and press seams flat.
3. Glue or sew trim on as you like!

56. children's nursery pictures

A simple project for those whose talents don't include sewing. It takes a little paint, a bit of cutting and a light hand with the glue pot.

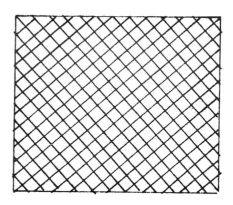

Materials

1. Simple unpainted wooden picture frames with glass, from the dime store (7 inches by 9 inches or 8 inches by 10 inches)
2. Lacquer paint (spray or brush type)
3. Gingham, calico or other childlike fabric
4. Children's classic picture books, e.g., Raggedy Ann, Beatrix Potter's animals or Kate Greenaway. (Cut out pictures that would be appropriate for framing.) If you have a talented artist in your group, you might have her do large watercolor letters of the alphabet.
5. Elmer's Glue or Sobo, thinned with water
6. Wire and picture hooks

How to

1. Spray or paint frames. Let dry.
2. Glue fabric to cardboard backing.
3. Center picture on fabric and glue on.
4. Finish with glass and frame.
5. Add a clean sheet of paper to cover back. Glue.
6. Attach hooks and wire for hanging.

57. sewing caddy

I am always looking for ways to get teen-agers turned on to sewing. I believe in a first effort being something like a long gathered skirt, or a patchwork quilt, or even this sewing caddy. It's a constant reminder to a new home sewer that she did it herself when it hangs so attractively on her bedroom wall.

Materials

1. Navy canvas: 21½ inches by 25½ inches
2. Red print pockets: 13 inches by 8½ inches; 7½ inches by 4½ inches; 6½ inches by 4½ inches
3. Green canvas pockets: 7½ inches by 8 inches; 6½ inches by 7 inches; 6½ inches by 4 inches
4. Red canvas pockets: 14 inches by 8½ inches; 6½ inches by 4 inches
5. Three 60-inch yellow tape measures (or ribbon woven to look like a yellow tape measure)
6. 1 yard inch-wide green grosgrain ribbon
7. 1 yard press-on Pellon

How to

1. Take navy canvas and iron on a backing of press-on Pellon. Turn navy edges under ½ inch and top-stitch.
2. Turn tops of all pockets ¼ inch under and top-stitch down. Pin and baste pockets on according to sketch, overlapping raw edges. (Leave slack in pockets for holding items.) Pin and baste center green square on. Stitch all pockets on.
3. Sew ribbon on to hold spools of thread by vertically top-stitching it down on sewing caddy.
4. Top-stitch all tape measures according to sketch. Hang via small rings sewn on back of sewing caddy.

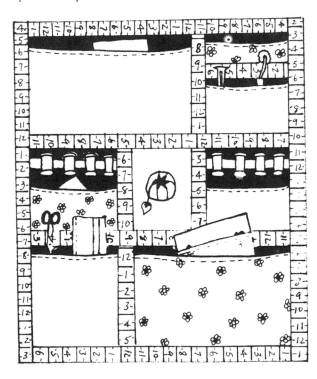

58. child's dress

This is a simple dress based on the night-gown pattern in the Ladies' Booth. The charm here is the imaginative use of fabrics. We suggest a blue calico print for the body of the dress, a yellow calico for the sleeves and perhaps a red calico for the pocket. It fits a toddler size 4.

Materials

1. ¾ yard of 45-inch blue calico
2. ½ yard of yellow calico and a scrap of red calico
3. ⅔ yard of ½-inch bias tape
4. ½ yard of ¼-inch elastic

How to

1. Follow nightgown directions, making the dress 8½ inches shorter than the gown.
2. Turn in pocket ¼ inch on all sides. Press.
3. Pin pocket to front of dress as is shown and sew on. Make a 6-inch square of yellow calico for the pocket handkerchief.
4. Make red bias tape bows for center of neckline and sleeve edges.
5. Add one pretty little girl!

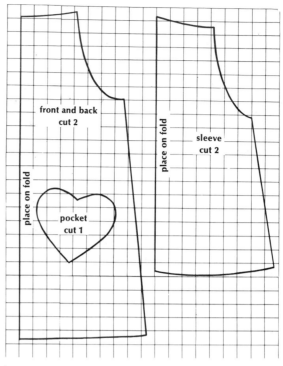

box = 1 sq. in.

126

59. child's place mat

A colorful and pleasant project to make and one that should be a good seller is a vinyl place mat for a young child. It visually teaches youngsters how to set their place at the table. It also washes clean easily because the materials are just brightly colored bits of oilcloth from the dime store.

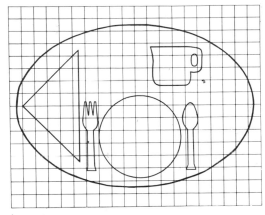

box = 1 sq. in.

Materials

1. Oilcloth or the cotton-backed vinyl used for kitchen tablecloths, 18 inches by 12 inches
2. Small pieces of contrasting colors, also in oilcloth or vinyl
3. 1½ yards double-fold bias tape
4. Iron-on interfacing
5. Elmer's Glue or Sobo

How to

1. Enlarge diagram and cut out pattern.
2. Scotch-tape the pattern to the vinyl or oilcloth and cut out. (Don't use pins, for the pin holes will show.)
3. *Note:* If the mat is only oilcloth, you may wish to back it with iron-on interfacing to give it additional body.
4. Finish off the edge of the mat with double-fold bias tape.
5. Glue the fabric utensils in place.

60. personalized plants for children

Here's a gift any child would adore that's not only fun, but educational as well!

Materials

1. Small clay flowerpots
2. Topsoil
3. Waterproof markers
4. Spray paint in a bright color
5. Packets of seeds
6. Plastic bag

How to

1. Spray-paint outside of pots. Allow to dry.

2. With marker write directly on each flowerpot the following:
   THIS PLANT BELONGS TO_____
   THIS IS AN_____PLANT
   DATE PLANTED_____
   DATE FIRST SPROUT APPEARED_____
   I MUST BE WATERED EVERY _____
                                       day, week, etc.

3. Sell each flowerpot with a plastic bag containing:
   One packet of seeds with instructions
   One packet of topsoil
   One marking pen

Note: Clay pots can also be left unpainted. Then start with step 2.

61. felt jump rope handles

Your imagination can play at this project. Felt jump rope handles are made to look like carrots, donkeys or giraffes—whatever you like.

Materials

1. Felt scraps
2. Clothesline rope ½ inch wide by 72 inches long

How to

1. Enlarge diagrams and cut out patterns.
2. Cut four carrots, giraffes, etc.
3. Cut out trim (four of each).
4. Pin leaves to carrots. Sew.
5. Pin two finished sides of carrot together, wrong sides facing each other.
6. Top-stitch around, ¼ inch from edge.
7. Fill in with cotton to give a "puffy" handle.
8. Slip handle over end of rope.
9. Stitch handle to rope by hand, concealing stitches where possible.

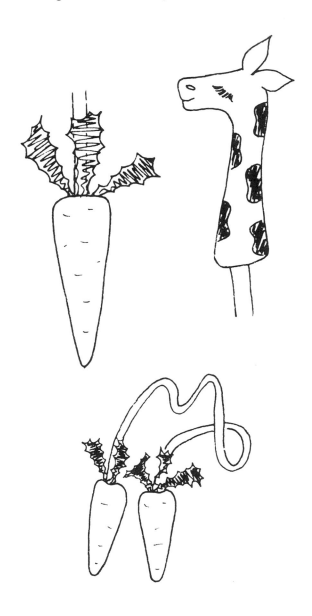

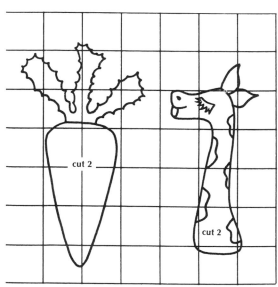

cut 2

cut 2

box =1 sq. in.

62. barbie doll sleeping bag

What self-respecting Barbie doll would be without her own sleeping bag? To solve her dilemma, set your volunteers to sewing these little quilted sleeping bags.

Materials

1. Cotton print fabric 13 inches by 9 inches
2. Lining in contrast color, 12 inches by 9 inches
3. Cotton batting for quilting
4. 4-inch zipper (or use smallest zipper you can find and cut it down to 4 inches)

How to

1. Make a "sandwich" of three fabrics, layering the quilt print on top, then batting and finally lining.
2. Pin through three layers.
3. Quilt the fabrics by machine, placing rows of machine stitching on the diagonal 1½ inches apart and using a large stitch.
4. Turn down a 1-inch hem on top side of quilt. Turn under ¼ inch to form finish on hem. Stitch with decorative zigzag stitch on machine.
5. Fold quilt in half lengthwise with right sides together. Pin.
6. Stitch bottom and side, leaving a 4-inch opening for zipper.
7. Baste this opening closed.
8. Press open side seam.
9. Place zipper flat on center of seam, right side down. Pin.
10. Stitch by hand, using a back stitch, ¼ inch from seam line.
11. Snip open basting at zipper line.
12. Cut off bottom corners to reduce bulk.
13. Open zipper and turn bag right side out.

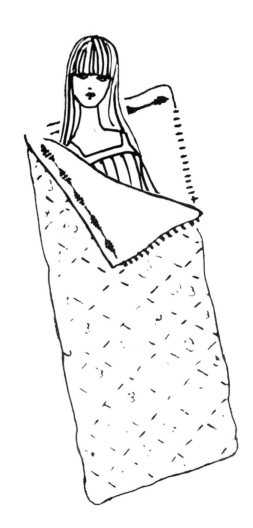

63. child's wall organizer

Here's a bright, colorful way to teach a child neatness. Make up a felt or canvas wall hanging with a variety of colored pockets to organize the ever-present clutter.

Materials

1. 36-inch square of heavy felt or canvas
2. 36-inch-long wooden ruler
3. Smaller pieces of felt or canvas in a variety of colors
4. Decorative braid or rope
5. Press-on Pellon, 36 inches square

How to

1. Press Pellon to back of canvas and hem edges.

2. Fold top back 2 inches.
3. Stitch a casing for rod 1¾ inches from edge.
4. Cut pockets in a variety of sizes. See diagram for suggestions.

Pockets:

5. Hem top of each pocket ¼ inch and stitch. Turn again ¼ inch and stitch.
6. Fold back sides ¼ inch and stitch.
7. Fold a pleat on each side of pocket and pin.
8. Turn up lower edge ¼ inch and stitch, catching side pleats while stitching.
9. Top-stitch to the backing fabric along inner pleat on sides and along the lower edge of pocket.

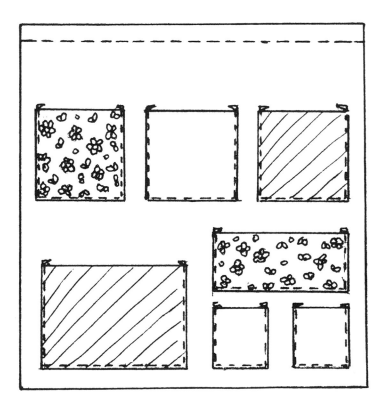

66. bandanna bib

Bandanna bib for young cowpokes is a quickie made from a bandanna and a terry washcloth.

Materials

1. White washcloth
2. Navy or red bandanna

How to

1. Cut bandanna diagonally in half.
2. From one triangle cut 1½-inch-wide bias strips.
3. Join strips and bind washcloth edges.
4. Top-stitch bandanna triangle to washcloth with its center point 5½ inches down from topedge of washcloth. Hem raw edge of bandanna to finish.

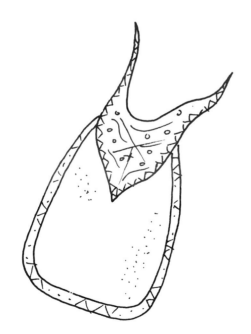

67. coffee can clown

There are so many things you can make out of a one-pound coffee can but I think this is one of the cleverest ideas I have seen in a long time. It's a clown that would be a good holder for a baby's cotton puffs or a dandy crayon box for a young child.

Materials

1. One 2-inch styrofoam ball
2. ⅓ yard small-print heavyweight fabric
3. Some pieces of different-color felt
4. Some flat rhinestones
5. ¼ yard white tulle
6. One empty 1-pound coffee can and two plastic lids
7. One small piece baby rickrack
8. One 1½-inch-long screw
9. Brown paper bag
10. Elmer's Glue or Sobo

How to

1. Cover outside of can (side only) with small-printed cotton fabric (use linen or canvas weight so glue won't show through). Glue fabric to can with Elmer's Glue diluted with water.
2. Cut the hat out of the same fabric, using hat pattern, then glue it to a piece of brown paper bag for added stiffness. Shape into a cone and glue to hold the shape.
3. Cut arms, hands, buttons and mouth out of colored felt. (Use different colors.) Then cut out two small circles for eyes and nose and a pair of thin strips for eyebrows. Glue *ends* of arms to side of can, leaving the center part free so that arms appear bent.

Glue hands and three large felt buttons as is pictured and then take three of the smaller felt buttons and glue them on top of the three large buttons. Glue a rhinestone on top of each finished button.

4. Take the 2-inch styrofoam ball and glue face parts on it. Glue hat on head. Take three remaining small felt buttons and glue on clown's hat down the center front, spaced evenly apart. You can add more glitter or felt trim here if you wish. Take a piece of baby rickrack and glue where styrofoam ball and hat meet to make a finished edge.

5. With hat, head and can finished, you are ready for the last step. Cut a 3-inch by 15-inch strip of nylon net or tulle and gather to make a ruff for the clown's head to sit upon. Take the screw, insert it through the center of the plastic lid of the coffee can and then through ruff and styrofoam ball. This holds head secure to lid. Take another plastic coffee can lid and snap it to bottom of coffee can to finish off the edge. Coffee can may be filled with cookies, candy, small gifts for children or adults.

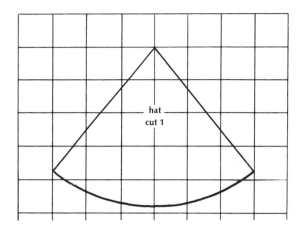

hat
cut 1

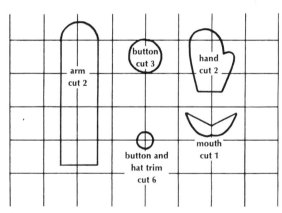

arm
cut 2

button
cut 3

hand
cut 2

button and
hat trim
cut 6

mouth
cut 1

box = 1 sq. in.

68. felt paper doll

A paper doll to please any little girl and really lots of fun to make. This is the time to go through your scrap boxes and dig out all your felt scraps and trims.

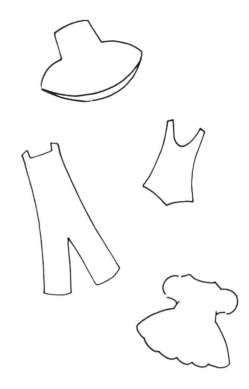

Materials

1. Felt in as many colors as possible
2. Felt-tipped marking pens
3. Yarn for hair
4. Trims such as net, lace, sequins, etc.
5. Cardboard

How to

1. Make patterns according to diagrams, out of cardboard.
2. Using cardboard pattern, cut doll out of pink felt. Glue on eyes of blue or brown felt. Mark mouth and cheeks with felt-tipped pen.
3. Sew or glue yarn on for hair.
4. Use imagination to cut out other clothes. Sew net ruffle to ballet dress, lace to a Sunday dress, etc.

box = 1 sq. in.

69. doll's patchwork quilt

Here's a little girl's version of granny's heirloom quilt. This could be a comfortable hand-sewn project for older volunteers or a machine project for your energetic go-getters. It's a great way to use up bits and pieces of old fabric scraps.

Materials

1. Lining fabric 16 inches by 22 inches
2. Ninety-six 2-inch squares, half print and half solid cotton
3. Quilt padding or baby flannel 13½ inches by 19½ inches (old receiving blankets can be cut to size)

How to

1. Sew small patches together eight across to form strips, using a ¼-inch seam allowance. Press seams open.
2. Join all rows, matching cross-seams. You can arrange squares to form any pattern you like.
3. Lay out lining. Cover with flannel and the patched cover.
4. Fold lining to front of cover, turning under ½ inch. Pin, miter corners. Sew on machine, catching patched pieces as you sew.

70. schoolbag organizer

What first-grader doesn't need a pocket for lunch money, bus pass, special signed papers and the all-important report card? This shoulder schoolbag organizer takes care of it all!

Materials

1. ¼ yard canvas
2. ¼ yard canvas in contrast color for lining
3. Two brass buttons
4. 3 yards bias binding

How to

1. Enlarge diagram and cut out pattern in canvas. Also, cut out a contrast-color lining in canvas, using the same pattern. Do for bag part only.
2. Cut out two canvas gusset strips 9 inches by 2½ inches.
3. Using a ¼-inch seam allowance, sew corresponding pocket flaps together, leaving bottom edges open. Turn, trim and press. Top-stitch around edges. Make a machine-made buttonhole in each pocket flap.
4. Turn under top edge of both pockets ½ inch and hem. Turn under three remaining edges of pockets ½ inch and top-stitch pockets onto one side of schoolbag organizer. Sew on pocket flaps and buttons to close.
5. Lay bag organizer on matching lining and top-stitch *all* edges together.
6. Finish off one end of each gusset with bias tape.
7. Fold bag in half and set gussets in either side. With finished ends of gussets toward top of bag, stitch sides and bottom of gussets to bag.
8. Finish off *all* edges of bag with bias binding.

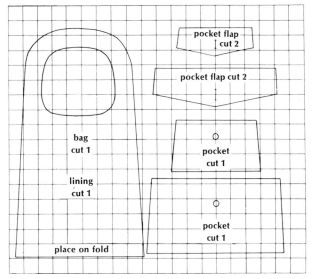

box = 1 sq. in.

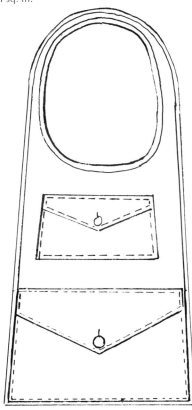

138

71. tortoise and hare place mat and bib

Favorite place mat and bib companions—
the tortoise and the hare—make mealtime a
fun time.

Materials for one set

1.   Two towels 12 inches by 18 inches
2.   Medium and baby rickrack
3.   Matching double-fold bias tape
4.   Scrap of terry cloth to match rickrack
and tape
5.   Fringe ball for tail
6.   Small button for eye

How to

1.   Enlarge diagrams and cut out patterns.
2.   Apply baby and medium rickrack to turtle as is sketched.
3.   Bind off edges with double-fold bias tape.
4.   Tack on small button for eye.
5.   On bib, appliqué hare from terry-cloth scrap.
6.   Use fringe ball for tail, double-fold bias tape for post and small fabric scrap for "Finish" sign.
7.   Bind around bib edge with double-fold bias tape as well as neckline edge, leaving a 15-inch extension on either end for ties.

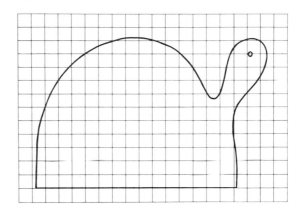

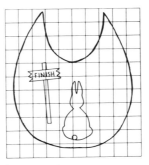

box = 1 sq. in.

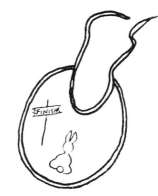

139

72. babies' building blocks

Soft washable squares for a baby's first building blocks. Good for your volunteers who enjoy hand sewing.

Materials

1. Oilcloth or vinyl-coated cotton for blocks. Bright colors and patterns.
2. Embroidery floss for contrast
3. Cotton batting for stuffing

How to

1. Cut 3-inch squares, six for each block.
2. Stitch together with embroidery floss, using blanket stitch.
3. Before completing, stuff firmly with cotton batting.
4. Package ten of these in cellophane bags tied with ribbon.

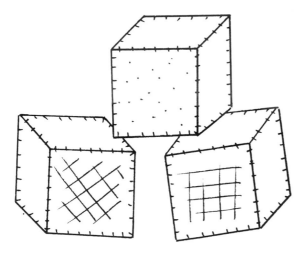

73. baby sling

Mothers everywhere are using the baby sling to keep their hands free for paying for groceries or for holding onto other wee ones. I think it's such a wonderful idea that how could I do a book without putting it in? And just look at how easy it is to make!

Materials

1. One piece of canvas 27 inches by 27 inches
2. One 2-inch-wide buckle

How to

1. Cut: 1 strap 21 inches by 5½ inches
         1 strap 27 inches by 5½ inches
         1 sling 20½ inches by 20 inches
2. Turn under a ½-inch hem on both 20½-inch sides of the sling. Then turn under ¼ inch again and top-stitch.
3. Starting 2 inches in, make pleats on outside of sling by folding along the lines in direction of the arrows as is illustrated (1). Baste each end to hold pleats until it is ready to be stitched to straps.
4. Turn under ½ inch on one side and one end of each strap and press. Do not stitch.
5. Then pin unpressed ends of straps to ends of baby sling, centering baby sling ends (2).
6. Wrap the strap edges around each end of the baby sling, overlapping flat edge over turned-under edge. Stitch across ends, using a 1½-inch seam allowance (3).
7. Turn straps right side out, folding turned-under edges of straps to flat edges

(4). Top-stitch at ends and down through center of both straps.

8.   Fasten buckle to free end of longer strap.

9.   Diagonally turn under the free end of the shorter strap and stitch down.

10. Insert strap through buckle and try on sling to adjust length. Stitch the diagonal end of the shorter strap down to other strap to hold straps stationary.

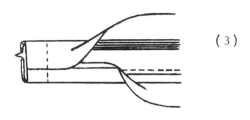

(3)

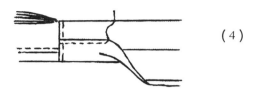

(4)

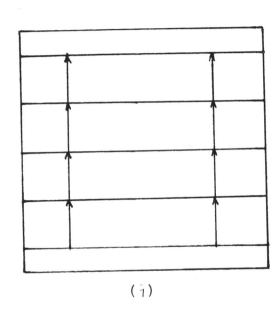

(1)

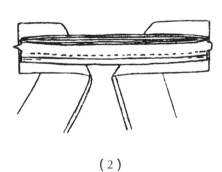

(2)

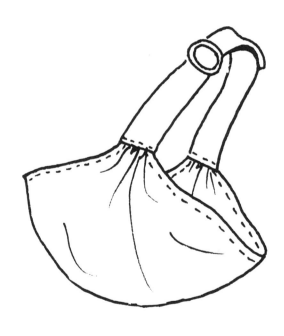

74. children's costumes

Think what fun a volunteer group would have creating literally a "bag of tricks" for children's favorite make-believe games. Simple costumes bagged attractively in plastic and tied with bright ribbons would be a great addition to a toy booth.

Materials

Fabric scraps, a selection of trims, press-on interfacings

How to

Princess—Gather 2 yards of net to a 1-inch-wide yard of ribbon. You might trim this skirt with sequins or glitter. A crown is a must! Cut one of cardboard and cover with satin or gold foil. To wear over a body leotard.

Nurse—A white bib apron with a red cross. An armband of white, another red cross and of course a nurse's cap: cut it out of lightweight cardboard and cover with white fabric. Add that red cross to front.

Red Riding Hood—Cut out a red fabric hood. Gather 2 yards of the same fabric for the cape. A small basket for grandmother's goodies completes the costume.

Pirate—A black patch sewn to a piece of elastic. Make a short vest from black cotton or felt. A print tricorner scarf to tie around the head—and of course a sword: cover a piece of cardboard with silver foil to make a blade. A nice touch—one gold hoop earring.

Doctor—An man's old white shirt can be cut off straight at shirttails and hem. Cut off cuffs. Hem. Cut off collar and add a small standing collar. Shirt can be buttoned up the back. Make a cardboard band with large round circle for head.

Indian—A headdress of real feathers would be great, but a felt headband trimmed with geometric felt shapes and a lone feather will do the job. For a loincloth, make two 12-inch squares of felt or suede cloth. Fringe bottom and attach one in front and one in back to a 1½-inch ribbon waistband. Attach a giant snap to close.

princess

nurse

red riding hood

pirate

doctor

indian

143

christmas booth

No color thought went into this booth at all but we did add red and green prints to the solids and of course lots of gold and silver glitter. I didn't want anybody left out, so the Christmas booth is for everybody—neighbors, newly made friends, shopkeepers, Sunday school teachers, mailmen, dentists, doctors, piano teachers and of course *you.*

75. advent calendar

This Advent calendar may make waiting for Christmas a little easier. Children eat one candy a day from the calendar, starting December 1, and before you can say Santa Claus it will be time to ring the bell—providing all the candy isn't eaten in the first two days!

Materials

1.   One green vinyl strip (with backing) 6¼ inches wide and 37 inches long
2.   One green vinyl circle 6¼ inches in diameter
3.   Heavy white construction paper
4.   3 yards red ribbon ¼ inch wide
5.   Twenty-four peppermint candies
6.   Sobo or Elmer's Glue
7.   Hole punch
8.   One 1-inch bell per calendar
9.   ⅓ yard of 1-inch-wide red-and-green plaid ribbon
10.   3 yards narrow red bias tape

How to

1.   Trim vinyl strip at both ends to form rounded edges.
2.   Sew bias tape around edge of vinyl circle.
3.   Cut one construction paper circle 5½ inches in diameter.
4.   Copy Advent poem onto paper circle, using colored ink.
5.   Glue paper circle to vinyl circle. Allow to dry. Then glue vinyl circle to top of long vinyl strip.
6.   Sew bias tape around entire strip plus attached circle.

7.   Punch two holes 1 inch apart in center of calendar, starting 3 inches up from the bottom. Continue punching a pair of holes every 2 inches along strip as is pictured.
8.   Cut the ¼-inch-wide red ribbon into 4-inch lengths and thread through holes, tying peppermint candies onto the calendar.
9.   Add one plaid bow at top and one at bottom of calendar. Lastly, attach a bell to bottom bow to ring when all the candies are gone and Christmas is here!

ADVENT POEM

December first to Christmas
  is the longest time of year.
Seems as though old Santa
  never will appear.

How many more days till Christmas
  it's so very hard to count.
So this little candy ribbon
  will tell the exact amount.

Untie a candy every night
  when the sandman casts his spell.
And Christmas Eve will be here
  by the time you reach
    THE BELL!

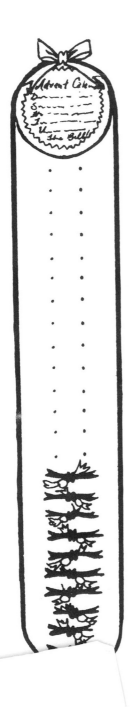

76. bow christmas wreath

Talk about a winner! This has got to be it. Just bag a bunch of ribbon bows and sell to decorate a wreath. If anybody complains about being "all thumbs," just tell her this project was custom-made for her.

Materials

1. 6 yards of 1½-inch-wide taffeta plaid ribbon, each yard being a different plaid pattern
2. One yard of 2-inch-wide plaid ribbon
3. One spool of thin wire

How to

1. Make one large bow out of the 2-inch-wide ribbon.
2. Make two bows out of each yard of the 1½-inch-wide ribbon.
3. Cut off a 4-inch piece of wire and attach to back of bow at each knot, or sell spool along with bag of ribbons for a do-it-yourself project.

77. christmas stocking

Be as creative as you like! This 19-inch-long felt Christmas stocking is decorated and appliquéd with any trimmings or findings you may have. No two are ever alike!

Materials

1. ¼ yard of felt makes two stockings
2. Scraps of assorted bias tape, rickrack, braid and ribbon for trim

How to

1. Enlarge diagram and cut out pattern.
2. Cut a 1-inch by 6-inch strip for hanging loop.
3. Arrange trimmings in bands all across one stocking piece and stitch in place.
4. With right sides facing, stitch both stocking pieces together with a ¼-inch seam, leaving top open. Clip curves and turn.
5. Make a 1-inch top hem.
6. Fold loop strip in half lengthwise, and top-stitch. Form loop and sew ends to inside back seam of stocking.

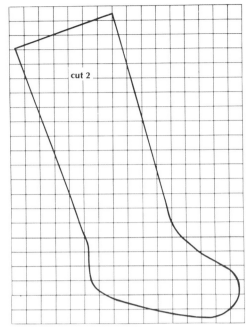

cut 2

box = 1 sq. in.

150

78. coffee can santa claus

Who would ever have thought there would be so many uses for an empty one-pound coffee can? Here it is all done up as a Santa Claus. Could be filled with homemade candy or cookies.

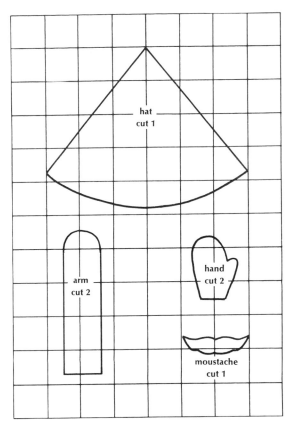

box = 1 sq. in.

Materials

1. One empty 1-pound coffee can and plastic lid
2. One 8-inch by 20-inch piece of red felt
3. Scraps of white and black felt, cotton (optional), white tulle, two pompons, narrow black grosgrain ribbon and buckle and a bell
4. One 2-inch styrofoam ball
5. One 1½-inch-long screw
6. Elmer's Glue or Sobo, thinned with water

How to

1. Measure can and cut out red felt to cover it completely. Glue felt on can.
2. Cut out arms, hands, hat.
3. Glue both *ends* of arms, hands, pompons, belt and buckle on can as is pictured.
4. Sew hat to form a triangle, attach bell to end and glue onto styrofoam ball. Cut out and glue on eyes, mustache and nose to ball. A bit of cotton for a beard and to trim hat can be added.
5. Make a ruff of a 2½-inch-wide strip of tulle to go under styrofoam ball head.
6. Punch a hole in the center of the plastic lid. Push the screw through the underside of the lid, going through the ruff and then through the bottom of the styrofoam ball head. Place lid on can to complete the coffee can Santa Claus.

79. christmas towel apron

Anyone who's busy working in a kitchen always needs to dry her hands on something and that something can be the towel apron. Make it up in Christmas green felt with a bright red hand towel or in any color combination that will look attractive enough to sell and sell and sell!

Materials

1. Felt yardage 38 inches by 26 inches for apron
2. Small fingertip terry-cloth hand towel
3. Two yards jumbo-sized gold or silver rickrack

How to

1. Cut apron pieces according to diagram.
2. Turn under apron skirt sides and bottom edge 2 inches and hem. Topstitch rickrack on right side of apron 2 inches in from edge on three sides as is sketched.
3. Cut off fringe of fingertip towel at one end. Pin to apron at upper edge according to sketch.

4. Gather edge including towel.
5. Fold waistband in half and sew to apron, leaving ends open.
6. Insert ties in these ends and sew securely.

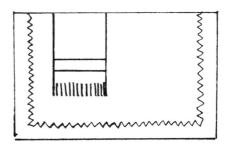

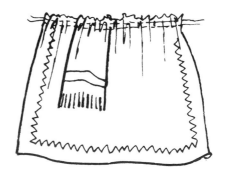

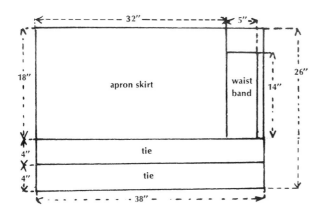

80. decorated straw baskets with homemade goodies

Anybody would like to receive a gift of homemade preserves, candies, cookies or cakes, especially if it's in a straw basket lined with a bright-colored reversible bread warmer. Volunteers who are absolute klutzes with a needle and thread could shine and sparkle with chocolate chips and chopped pecans!

Materials

1. Baskets—all shapes and sizes; best with handles though not necessary
2. Christmas red and green in cotton solids and prints that complement each other

How to

1. Measure entire inside of basket and cut out a pattern to fit.
2. Cut one each of two different fabric patterns that go well together or one solid and one print for each basket.
3. Place right sides together.
4. Sew a 1-inch seam, leaving a 2-inch opening.
5. Trim seams, clip curves.
6. Turn, press and slip-stitch opening closed.
7. Line basket. Trim with a bright-red bow. Fill with homemade goodies and watch how fast it sells!

81. bandanna bag

This handy bag you can make in a jiffy because it's nothing more than one bandanna
folded and stitched around *two* bracelets!

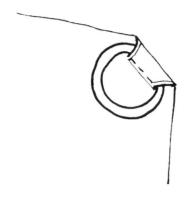

Materials

  1. 22-inch-square bandanna (or scarf)
  2. Two plastic bangle bracelets

How to

  1. Measure 10 inches along both sides
of a corner of the scarf and mark these two
points with pins.
  2. Lay a bracelet on the scarf in this corner.
  3. Turn the tip of the corner under 1
inch and bring this squared-off flap over the
bracelet and pin as shown. Stitch, making a
casing approximately ¾ inch wide.
  4. Repeat with opposite corner.
  5. With right sides of the purse together,
lay the bracelets and the side edges on top
of each other.
  6. Pin the sides of the purse together
and stitch from the marker pins to the corner.
  7. Turn bag right side out and poke corners until bottom of bag is squared off.

82. fabric-covered mirrors or picture frames

These can add color and pattern interest to a room. The picture frames also make lovely gifts for parents or grandparents. Just add a child's school picture and watch the smiles all around.

Materials

1. Plain wooden or cardboard frame with glass (best buys are found in the dime store)
2. Fabric the size of frame plus 1 inch all around: heavy cotton works best
3. Sobo or Elmer's Glue
4. Matching or contrasting fabric to cover back of frame

How to

1. Remove backing and glass from frame.
2. Lay frame right side down on fabric, i.e., wrong side up.
3. Cut fabric away from outside corners as in diagram.
4. Spread a length of glue along outer rim of back of frame (A in diagram), doing one side at a time.
5. Wrap material around frame, making sure it's taut.
6. Press fabric with fingers until it begins to stick to the frame. Let this dry. Do same for other three sides.
7. Then, using sharp scissors, cut away fabric on the inside of frame, leaving a 1-inch border all around.
8. Spread white glue along inside rim of back of frame (B in diagram), doing one side at a time.
9. Press fabric until it sticks. Let dry. Do other three sides.
10. Glue braid on to finish off edge or cover back of frame with a matching or contrasting fabric.

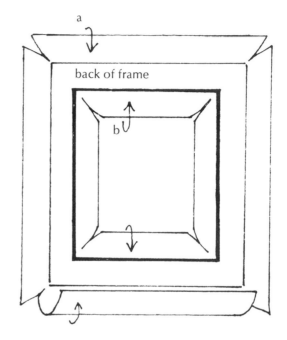

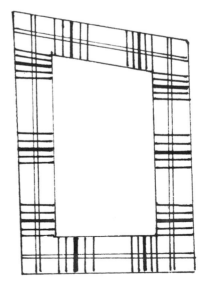

155

83. guest hand towel

Christmas guest towels, easy to make and a thoughtful gift for friends who entertain frequently.

Materials

1. Good quality red terry cloth fingertip towels, two or three to a set
2. ½-inch-wide eyelet lace in which to thread ribbon
3. Green velvet ribbon ¼ inch wide and approximately 20 inches long

How to

1. Measure lace the width of towel. Pin on at one end of towel 2 inches up from fringed edge.
2. Turn eyelet lace ends under ½ inch at either side of towel. Top-stitch on.
3. Cut green velvet ribbon in half. Then, starting from either end of eyelet lace, thread ribbon through it and tie in a small bow at the center.

84. paperback book cover

Choose a paperback book as a gift and then make a book cover for it! Use any washable fabric and then make a bright-colored felt hair-clip bookmark to go with it.

Materials

1. ¼ yard any fabric (except for heavy wools)
2. Cotton fabric for lining

How to

1. Cut fabric to fit size of entire outside of book plus a ¼-inch seam allowance. Be sure to measure each paperback before cutting cover, as they vary in thickness and size.
2. Cut a lining that is 12 inches wider than the cover.
3. Fold each end of the lining 3 inches in to what would be the center of the book. Then fold again 3 inches, forming a finished pocket flap. Pin and baste.
4. With right sides together, stitch cover and lining together, leaving a 4-inch opening for turning. Turn; stitch closed.
5. Slip cover onto book.

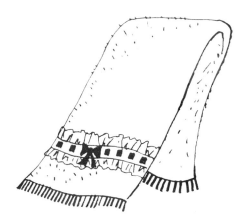

85. hair-clip bookmark

You never know when you'll come across a most unusual idea, and this is certainly one of them. I was visiting my Aunt Babe (we all call her Aunt Babe even though her real name is Wilhemina Elizabeth, and if you find that strange, she has a sister named Elizabeth Wilhemina, whom we all call Aunt Sis) and she brought out some items that had made money at her bazaar and that's how I found the hair-clip bookmark!

Materials

1. One 8-inch-square piece of colored felt
2. ¼ yard of ½-inch-wide lace
3. One 1½-inch-long hair clip

How to

1. Cut four "mittens" of solid-color felt according to pattern given.
2. Hand-whip together a pair of mittens as is pictured, leaving bottom edge open for one side of hair clip.
3. Whip together the other pair the same way and then sew a ½-inch bit of gathered lace around end of both pairs of mittens, being careful not to close the openings for the hair clip.
4. Hold them together by inserting one side of hair clip in one mitten and the other side of hair clip in the other mitten. Clip onto page of book to keep your place.

86. sewing pocket belt

Handy sewing pocket of felt has tape measure belt that holds pincushion, scissors and other notions right on hand when you need them.

Materials

1. ⅓ yard felt
2. One 60-inch yellow tape measure
3. One round red (tomato) pincushion
4. Pins, scissors
5. ½ yard double-fold bias tape

How to

1. Enlarge diagram and cut out pattern.
2. Cut: a 14-inch length of bias tape for pocket edge;
    a scissors loop 1 inch by 3 inches in felt;
    a belt strip 2½ inches by 60 inches in felt.
3. Stitch bias tape to inside curved edge of pocket piece B.
4. With right sides together, stitch B to A around outer edge. Clip edges and turn.
5. Fold scissors strip in half lengthwise and stitch along edges through both thicknesses; pin ends to top part of pocket, forming loop as shown.
6. Fold belt in half lengthwise. Insert pocket to the right of the center of the belt and top-stitch entire length of belt.

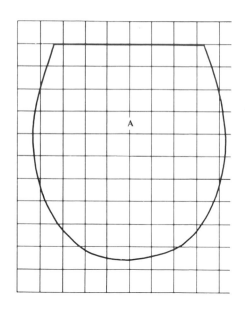

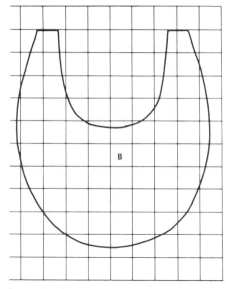

box =1 sq. in.

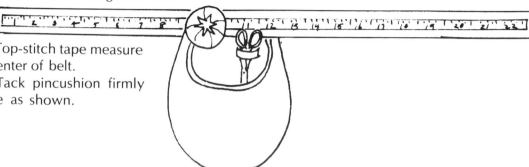

7. Top-stitch tape measure along center of belt.
8. Tack pincushion firmly in place as shown.

158

87. scissors caddy

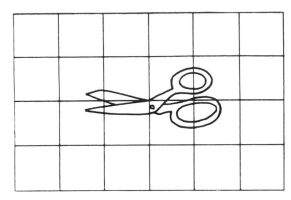

box = 1 sq. in.

Who would believe that upholstery webbing could make such an attractive wall caddy? One thing is for sure: you'll never misplace a pair of scissors again!

Materials

1.   1 yard of 3½-inch-wide upholstery webbing
2.   Scraps of red and green felt
3.   Small ring for hanging

How to

1.   Cut a piece of webbing 20 inches long. Cut another piece 10 inches long.
2.   Cut out a scissors design in both red and green felt.
3.   On the long piece of webbing, turn back the corners at one end and hand-stitch down. Sew on ring for hanging.
4.   Turn under one end of short piece of webbing 2 inches and place this end on top of long piece of webbing 5 inches down from ring. Then turn up the other end of the long piece over the short, fold edge under and top-stitch both sides down.
5.   Glue on cut-out scissors as is shown.
6.   Lastly, type up a little note and insert in scissors caddy. The note should read:

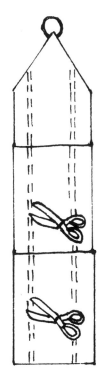

> This is for your scissors
> Be they large or small
> Here you'll always find them
> If you hang this on the wall.

159

88. ribbon clutch purse

I saw this idea in Paris one day in a little boutique on the Left Bank and thought it perfect for a home sewer to duplicate. It's just a few ribbons, a scrap of velvet and a little time!

Materials

1. Enough 1-inch-(or ½-inch-) wide ribbons to weave a rectangle 10 inches by 14 inches. Use a variety of colors in all satin ribbons but maintain the same width ribbon
2. One piece of velvet or velveteen 10 inches by 7½ inches
3. One piece of taffeta 10 inches by 14 inches
4. One piece of taffeta 10 inches by 7½ inches
5. One piece of interfacing 10 inches by 14 inches
6. One button

How to

1. With wrong sides together, sew the 7½-inch pieces of taffeta and velveteen together, using a ½-inch seam allowance and leaving a 4-inch opening. Turn and press, using a velvet board. Slip-stitch opening closed.
2. Pin the ribbons (interweaving them) on the interfacing, top-stitching around edge to hold at one 10-inch end, to form a point, and top-stitch to that point to form outside point of bag.
3. With the ribbon side and the 10-inch by 14-inch piece of taffeta facing each other, sew around edge, using a ½-inch seam allowance and leaving a 4-inch open-ing. Trim corners, turn and press. Slip-stitch opening closed.

4. Slip-stitch both the velvet and the ribbon pieces together, leaving the top edge of the velvet open. Fold pointed ribbon edge down over velvet edge and sew on a button and a piece of thin round elastic to close.

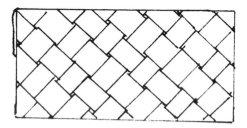

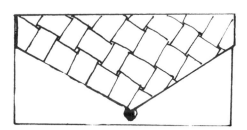

89. watermelon eyeglass case

Here's a whimsical sunglass or eyeglass case that would make a delightful gift for a child or a teenager. It can even double as a charming little purse.

Materials

1. Scraps of green, red, white, black felt
2. 9-inch zipper
3. Elmer's Glue or Sobo

How to

1. Enlarge diagram and cut pattern.
2. Cut two each of large rind from green, small rind from white and inner portion from red. Cut five or six seeds for each side. (*Note:* You can cut one side as directed and make back a solid color, if you want to simplify it.)
3. Appliqué white rind onto green, using decorative stitch on sewing machine.
4. Appliqué red portion onto white, forming watermelon as shown. Repeat for other side.
5. Place right side top edge of watermelon along right side of zipper tape; pin; stitch.
6. Repeat for other side.
7. Fold so that the right sides of the watermelon face each other.
8. Open zipper.
9. Join curved edge of both watermelon sections and stitch, using a ¼-inch seam allowance.
10. Turn right side out. Glue seeds onto each side.

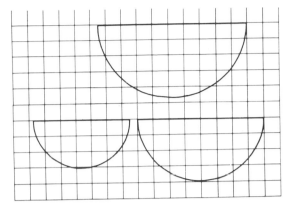

box = 1 sq. in.

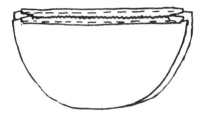

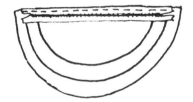

161

90. neck roll cover

A stiff neck will be a thing of the past with this charming neck roll. It's an easy-to-sew project with straight seam cutting and sewing. So get out all your beginner sewers for this one!

Materials

1. Piece of gingham or other fabric 20 inches by 18 inches
2. 1 yard of 1½-inch-wide cotton lace
3. 1 yard of 1 ¾-inch-wide *ruffled* cotton lace
4. 1½ yards of ½-inch-wide satin ribbon

How to

1. Top-stitch one edge of lace to raw edge of ruffled lace. Cut this strip in half.

2. Measure in 4½ inches from both ends of gingham piece and mark with pins. Baste edge of each lace strip to this pin marking. Top-stitch both edges of lace down, leaving lace ruffle free as is shown in sketch.

3. Make a ½-inch casing in both ends of gingham piece.

4. Fold gingham piece in half lengthwise with right sides together. Sew raw edges together. Turn and press.

5. With tip of scissors, make a hole in each casing. Cut ribbon in half and insert one strip of ribbon in each casing.

6. Have one neck roll cover with a neck roll pillow inside at the booth to show the finished product. However, sell it with the customer to supply the pillow herself.

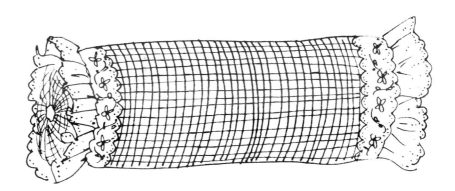

91. exercise mat

I think this is a great incentive to exercise (is there anybody who *likes* doing exercises?) or simply to have at a pool or patio for relaxing.

Materials

1. 4 yards printed or solid quilted cotton
2. 6 yards wide bias tape in contrast color
3. 2 yards matching tape or ribbon for ties

How to

1. Cut two panels of quilted cotton 72 inches by 30 inches.
2. With wrong sides facing, pin panels together through center.
3. Stitch panels together on all four sides.
4. Bind edges with bias tape, mitering corners.
5. On back, stitch center of ribbon or tape 12 inches from either the top or bottom edge.
6. Roll up mat and tie ribbon or tape in a bow when you've finished doing all those exercises!

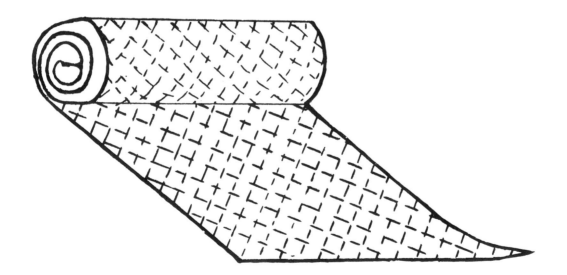

94. apple place mat and napkin

Charming apple place mat and colorful napkin will delight any child at mealtime.

Materials for one

1. ½ yard quilted calico fabric
2. ½ yard coordinating sailcloth (solid)
3. ½ yard bias tape and scrap of matching cording

How to: Place mat

1. Enlarge diagram for apple. Cut one from quilted fabric and one from sailcloth.
2. Pin these two sections with right sides together.
3. Stitch all around, using a ¼-inch seam allowance and leaving an opening at top.
4. Clip all curves. Turn. Press.
5. Insert 2-inch length of cording in top of apple for stem. Top-stitch all around mat ¼ inch from edge, catching stem in stitching.
6. Fold bias tape in double loop as shown and tack onto front over stem.

How to: Napkin

1. Cut a 10-inch square from sailcloth and round off corners.
2. Bind all around with contrasting bias tape.

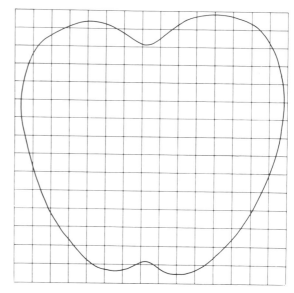

box = 1 sq. in.

95. ribbon matchbooks

A miniature basket of matchbooks covered in Christmas striped ribbon. A stocking stuffer or pretty table accessory.

Materials

1. Small green straw baskets, 2½ inches long, found in dime stores
2. Ribbon 1½ inch wide, striped in red and white, 5 inches long for each matchbook
3. Plain matchbooks
4. Elmer's Glue or Sobo, diluted with water

How to

1. Simply cut ribbon into 5-inch lengths. Glue them to the outside of the matchbook covers.
2. Stuff four or five covered matchbooks tightly into a basket. Dime-store-variety tiny flowerpots can be filled with matchbooks too!

96. ribbon tape measure

A nice addition to the contents of any handbag, especially needed when going on a home decorating spree or a reminder when the pounds start making their home *chez vous!*

Materials

1. One 36-inch-long tape measure
2. 38 inches of 1-inch-wide grosgrain ribbon
3. One snap

How to

1. Top-stitch tape measure in center of ribbon.
2. Fold over a 2-inch piece of ribbon and hand-sew onto beginning end of ribbon tape measure. Sew snap on folded-over piece of ribbon ends. Fold up tape measure (fold every 3 inches) and close by snapping folded-over piece of ribbon ends together.

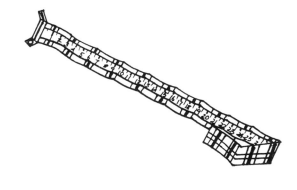

97. coffee can christmas boot

This idea came my way because a very dear aunt (the one named Elizabeth Wilhemina, whom we all call Aunt Sis) has arthritis and she needs to keep her fingers active, so—talk about a doer!—she made two-hundred of these and turned all the money over to the Arthritis Foundation! See what you can do if you just look around!

Materials

1. ¼ yard red felt
2. One 1-pound coffee can and plastic lid
3. ½ yard gold lace or braid, ½ inch wide
4. Six gold metal eyelets
5. ½ yard thin gold cord
6. One 8-inch-square lightweight cardboard
7. One 1-inch round gold drawer knob and screw purchased in hardware store

How to

1. Enlarge diagram and cut all pattern pieces out of red felt. Sew together, matching up numbers. Make only a ¼-inch seam and sew wrong sides together. (Do not turn over but let seam stitching show on the outside.)
2. Sew on ½-inch-wide gold lace or braid to finish off top of boot.
3. Punch in metal eyelets and lace up with gold cord as is pictured.
4. Cut out a cardboard ''sole'' and insert inside boot bottom so it will sit flat on a table.
5. Glue the red felt circle to the top of the plastic coffee can lid.

6. For a handle on the lid, take a 1-inch round gold knob and screw it through the plastic lid and red felt lid cover. (Punch a hole with an ice pick or point of scissors in the center of the lid, to facilitate screwing on the knob.)
7. Fill with Christmas candy or cookies.

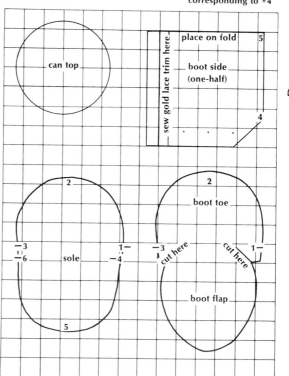

box = 1 sq. in.

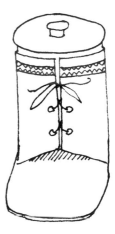

168

98. christmas package name tags

Here's a great idea for wrapping and tagging small Christmas packages. The brightly colored paper name tags are stapled to a ½-inch-wide gold piece of elastic so that you tie and tag your package all in one!

Materials for three name tags

1. Scraps of brightly colored heavy-weight construction paper
2. 1 yard of ½-inch-wide gold elastic
3. Staple gun
4. Glue
5. Plastic bag

How to

1. Cut out two of each design in the construction paper.
2. Taking only one of each design, staple a 10-inch piece of elastic to back. Staple both ends of elastic to this design to form a circle of elastic so that it will go around a package.
3. Using glitter, marking pens, gold braid, cotton or whatever you have around, decorate one side of each of the other designs, remembering to leave enough open space for names. Glue these decorated designs on top of their corresponding half.
4. Put three designs in a bag and sell.

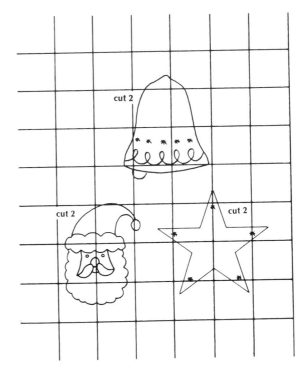

box = 1 sq. in.

169

99. soft handbag

An easy-to-make handbag that came about
because a relative was on crutches for quite
a while and she complained about her regular handbags rubbing her wrist when she
used the crutches. She devised the soft
handbag, which took care of the problem
and was decorative as well. It's been made
to go into the Christmas booth but any design and color combination would work as
well.

Materials

  1.   ½ yard green felt
  2.   10-inch by 10-inch square of white
felt
  3.   Scraps of red felt
  4.   1¼ yards each medium-size red and
white rickrack
  5.   Silver and red sequins

How to

  1.   Enlarge diagram and cut out pattern.
  2.   Cut out the snowflake design in white
felt. Use your imagination to cut any additional diamonds or circles in the snowflake
itself. Then topstitch it onto one side of the
soft handbag. Sew on a few small felt circles
as well as red and silver sequins by hand.
  3.   With right sides facing, sew the two
handbag pieces together. Use a ½-inch
seam allowance and sew around bottom
sides and top, leaving curved edges open.
  4.   Trim seams; turn and press.
  5.   Baste the curved edges under ½ inch
and top-stitch down.
  6.   Lastly, top-stitch on the two rows of
rickrack as is shown in sketch.

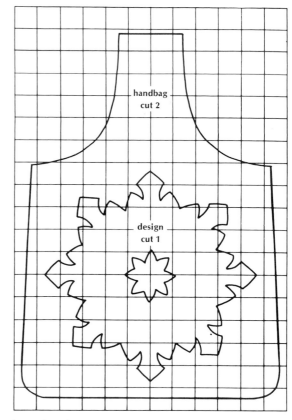

box = 1 sq. in.

100. round christmas tablecloth

This is a tablecloth that can be used *any* time of the year but it looks especially festive in red and green for that time of the year when Santa comes.

Materials

Bright red cotton, corduroy, felt or velveteen. Yardage needed is according to the size of the table.

How to

1. Measure table from center of top to floor. This will give the radius of the circle. You will have to piece the circle because it will be impossible to purchase fabric that is wide enough. Measure carefully *before* you purchase fabric. If you have a bold print or plaid, purchase extra fabric so that you can match it.

2. The amount measured from center of table to floor plus hem (2 inches recommended) *quadrupled* will give you the amount of basic yardage. For example, if your table is 50 inches from center to floor, purchase four times that amount plus 8 inches more. Remember, for a 50-inch center-to-floor table you want a piece of fabric folded in quarters that measures 52 inches on the fold lines. See drawing for a 50-inch cloth.

3. Left fold line should measure required inches *after* sewing seam.

4. Place measuring tape at what will be the center of the cloth. Carefully pin or mark along fabric where the center-to-floor measurement will be.

5. Pin fabric together so that your cutting line will be the same for all layers. If you are using heavy fabric, cut only one or two thicknesses at a time.

6. Sew and hem cloth.

7. This kind of tablecloth makes a great background for presents or, with a white or green square on top, is ready for dining.

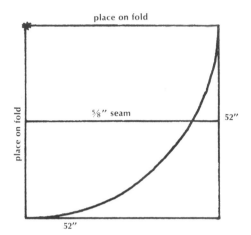

171

If you have an unusual or unique gift idea for our forthcoming bazaar book, send a sample and a pattern of it to:

FRANCINE COFFEY
The Singer Company
30 Rockefeller Plaza
New York, N.Y.10020

If your idea is used you will receive $10 and your name will be credited in the book. Unfortunately, we will not be able to return the samples.

notes

notes

notes

notes

notes

notes